DEVELOPING AWARENESS FOR THE TEACHING OF PEACE EDUCATION AMONG PROSPECTIVE TEACHERS

Developing Awareness for the Teaching of Peace Education Among Prospective Teachers

Dr Manish Bhatnagar

GYAN

ISBN: 978-81-212-1260-1

Price: ₹ 469/-

Published by

Gyan Books (P) Ltd.
Gyan Kunj, 23 Main Ansari Road
Daryaganj, Delhi – 110052
E-mail: books@gyanbooks.com
Ph.: 23282060, 23261060, Fax.:011&2328914

Laser Typesetting: Lucky Graphic, Delhi
Printed at: G. Print Process, Delhi

Cataloging in Publication Data—DK
Courtesy: D.K. Agencies (P) Ltd. <docinfo@dkagencies.com>

Bhatnagar, Manish, author.
Developing awareness for the teaching of peace education among prospective teachers / Dr Manish Bhatnagar.

pages cm
Includes bibliographical references (pages) and index.
ISBN 9788121212601
1. Peace—Study and teaching—India—Udaipur (Rajasthan)
2. Teachers—Training of—India—Udaipur (Rajasthan) I. Title.

DDC 327.1720710544 23

Contents

Preface

May there be peace.

The title of the research work is "Developing awareness for the teaching of peace education among prospective teachers." It is an attempt to develop peace culture in our prospective teachers and through them in our future citizens residing presently in the schools. The work mainly addresses principals, teacher educators and prospective teachers and inspires them to inculcate peace culture in their respective institutions.

The book is divided into five chapters. First chapter introduces the need, importance, development and meaning of peace education. It also deals with the objectives, role of schools and teachers in promoting peace education. The second chapter is devoted to review the related literature available in this area. The third chapter presents research design mainly preparation of teaching package, tools and techniques applied. The fourth chapter deals with the data collection, tabulation, analysis and interpretation of data. The fifth and final chapter concludes the research work.

Concluding Thoughts

Orientation programme is an integral part of our teacher education institutions. The view of the researcher is that this work is a guide to the teacher educators who aims to empower our prospective teachers in their attempt to foster peace values in them. However, teacher educators can build much more from their experiences gained through this approach in their classroom and the outer world.

It is my proud privilege to express a profound sense of gratitude and sincere indebtedness to my respected guide Prof. Hemlata Talesra, former Head, Department of Education, Jain Vishva Bharti University, Ladnun, for her precious guidance, expert advice, timely help, persistent encouragement, and inspiration that has been given to me.

I offer my thanks to the faculty members and library staff of UNESCO, NCERT, NUEPA and JNU, New Delhi for their due help and guidance.

I am equally grateful to the experts in the field of education who helped me with their valuable suggestions during the research period.

Patience and understanding shown by my family members is also thankfully acknowledged.

Last but not the least, I express my deep sense of gratitude to all the persons who directly or indirectly gave me their precious time and helped in the completion of this work.

MANISH BHATNAGAR

1

The Perspective

'Peace is possible for life at all stages and it is up to man to choose his destiny or to suffer from the horrors of war. Today mankind is at the cross-road where he has to choose with courage, determination and imagination.'

-Federico Mayor

1.1 Introduction

Violence is emerging in an unprecedented manner in human society. If we look at the world today we feel disheartened and even horrified to see the kind of violent acts being committed by man against man and nature. Today, we live in an era of unprecedented violence in the forms of terrorism, war, crimes, injustice and oppression and exploitation. The majority of mankind lives in stark poverty, struggling for bare survival. There is vast disorder and confusion in the society which has been created by man himself.

The saddest part of the story is that this state of disorder and confusion in the society is affecting the children's innocent minds. Today children are absorbing the spirit of violence in the atmosphere and our next generation is becoming perpetuators of violence. Therefore, the need of the hour is to nurture peace in the hearts of children.

Under the present predicament there is a growing realisation in the world of education today that children should be educated in the art of peaceful living. As a result, more and more peace concepts, attitudes, values and behavioural skills are being integrated into school curricula in many countries.

1.2 Development of Peace Education

In the past, peace education had been an integral part of education at all times and in all cultures, every culture regarded peace as a noble ideal to attain. However with the advent of western secularism at the beginning of the 20th century through the guise of a positivist scientific outlook to education, moral and human values including peace were slowly discouraged away from school curricula. Under the ideal of value-free positivist and reductionist knowledge the whole education was viewed narrowly as teaching facts of various subjects.

However, in spite of such materialistic views, the thinking of such humanists like Rousseau, Henry Thoreau, Tolstoy and Maria Montessori kept the sense of education alive. With the witness of the horrors of the First and Second World Wars there was a reawakening to the need of developing the humanistic side of education at least among a few educationists. In this context, Maria Montessori's loud and tireless reiteration on the need for educating for peace should be mentioned here with respect and appreciation. Today, we are only rediscovering her vision of peace education which she tried to tell the world in the 1930s. According to her, those who want war prepare young people for war; but those, who want peace, have neglected young, children and adolescents and as a result they are unable to organise them for peace. Her vision of education provides a meaningful sound basis for peace education. She looked at education as a tool for building World Peace. To her peace is the guiding principle of man and nature. Any attempt to deviate from the principle will only bring about destruction. However, it has never been investigated seriously so far. Peace should be studied as a science identifying its direct and indirect complex factors.

1.3 Development of Peace Education in Indian Context

As far as peace education in Indian context is concerned

peace education is not a new concept. Ancient Indian education system (in ashrams) promoted peace culture and all ancient Indian educators (Rishis in the ashrams) were peace educators.

1.3 (a) A Bird Eye View of Peace Education in Ancient Indian Education World

India has a long and vivacious history of promoting peace, international understanding, tolerance and self-restraint which are evident in the Vedas, Puranas and Upanishads. The ancient Indian Rishis visualised the Earth as a Global village. They visualised it as "*vasudaiva kutumbakam*" i.e., the whole world is a family.

Swami Vivekananda, the illustrious apostle of Sri Rama Krishna whose great mission was to preach mankind their divinity and to manifest it in every moment of life. Swami Vivekananda said that the ultimate aim of education is to establish internal peace and security by strengthening the spiritual foundations of different nations. He preached tolerance in religion and education which essentially lead to peace. He preached the universal brotherhood of mankind.

Srimanta Shanker Dev of Assam (1449 AD-1568 AD) not only propagated the new "Vaishanavism" in Assam but consolidated the foundation of the Assamese culture, music, literature and unified the people of diverse caste and community. He preached the principle of equality, compassion, love and brotherhood and boldly asserted in the Kirtan Ghosa the need of giving everyone equal status and dignity in the society.

Swami Chinmayananda was an ascetic of modern India who worked for over four decades spreading the vedantic message of peace and happiness to the classes and masses around the globe.

The thoughts and actions for promoting peace by outstanding personalities like Mahatma Gandhi, Md. Iqbal, and Rabindra Nath Tagore captivated the world's attention.

Living spiritual leaders of India like Sri Sri Ravi Shankar of Art of Living are the apostle of peace and harmony.

Acharya Mahapragya made efforts for spreading peace in the society and tried to unite people of various castes and religions. His "Ahinsa Yatra" was also an effort in this direction. His view on anekant also reflects the importance of peace education globally.

APJ Abdul Kalam, former President of India linked Nation's prosperity with peace. He referred the message received from a Buddhist Monk in a statement and said that, "If you want peace, remove 'I' and 'Me'. When you remove 'I' and 'Me', you remove ego. When you remove ego, you remove hatred. When you remove hatred, you have peace".

1.3 (b) Views Related to Peace Education in the Reports of Different Commissions and Committees Formed After Independence

Peace education as a slogan and in the form of a resolution was introduced in India in the document of National Curriculum Framework 2005 of NCERT. Many committees have gone into the question of how to foster healthy and positive value orientation. These include committee on Moral and Religious Instruction (1959-1960) and the committee on Emotional Integration (1961). These committees and many of our educational thinkers have laid stress on getting familiar with the teaching of great persons of all religions. In fact, Dr Radhakrishnan was a great believer in introducing moral education in our educational institutes. He suggested many recommendations in this regard in the report of University Education Commission (1948-1949). The main recommendations were compulsory morning prayer and introducing moral education in the first degree course. In the report of the Secondary Education Commission (1952-1953) and Indian Education Commission (1964-1966) we find some peace values in the forms of aims of education namely, education for total development of personality and education for social and moral values. The National Policy on Education (1986) has sections on value education for instance it states that (In our country with its multiple diversities), education should foster universal and eternal values towards integrating people by preserving unity in diversity, tolerance is to be fostered in students. Children must be made conscious of the environment and how to care for it, so as to utilise the advantages without destroying the asset. In this way we find some traces of peace education in the form of peace values for creating culture of peace in our institutions.

1.3 (c) Peace Education in the National Curriculum Framework for School Education

Comparative study of all religions should be included in curriculum. For this NCF 2000 formed an integrated approach. This also emphasised that value education and teaching of all religions should be included in the syllabus of different subjects.

1.3 (d) National Curriculum Framework (NCF) 2005

For the first time special emphasis is being presented in the National Curriculum Framework (NCF) 2005 on peace education.

Education for Peace

We live in an age of unprecedented levels of violence, with constant threats posed by intolerance, fanaticism, dispute and discordance. Ethical action, peace and welfare are facing new challenges. War and violence occur due to unresolved conflicts, though conflicts may not always lead to violence and war. Violence is one of the many possible responses to conflict. Non-violent conflict-resolution skills could be nurtured and applied constructively to resolve disputes between the individuals, groups and nations. The space for peace education within the framework of National School Curriculum document is compellingly clear in the light of escalating trends of, and taste for, violence globally, nationally and locally. Education is a significant dimension of the long-term process of building up peace – tolerance, justice, intercultural understanding and civic responsibility. However, education as practiced in schools often promotes forms of violence, both real and symbolic. Under these circumstances, the need to reorient education and therefore the school curriculum takes priority. As a value, it cuts across all other curricular areas, and coincides with and compliments the values emphasised therein.

It is, therefore, a concern cutting across the curriculum and is the concern of all teachers.

Education for peace seeks to nurture ethical development, inculcating the values, attitudes and skills required for living in harmony with oneself and with others, including nature. It embodies the joy of living and personality development with the qualities of love, hope and courage. It encompasses respect for human rights, justice, tolerance, co-operation, social responsibility, and respect for cultural diversity, in addition to a firm commitment to democracy and non-violent conflict resolution. Social justice is an important aspect of peace education. The concern for equality and social justice, which refers to practicing non-exploitation towards the have-nots, the poor and the underprivileged and creating a non-violent social system, is the hallmark of education for peace. Similarly, human rights are central to the concept of peace. Peace cannot prevail if the rights of individuals are violated. Basic to human rights are the values of non-discrimination and equality, which contribute to building a culture of peace in society. These issues are interrelated. Peace education is thus a host of overlapping values.

Peace education must be a concern that permeates the entire school life-curriculum, co-curriculum, classroom environment, school management, teacher-pupil relationship, teaching learning processes and the entire range of school activities. Hence, it is important to examine the curriculum and examination system from the point of view of how they may contribute to children's sense of inadequacy, frustration, impatience and insecurity. Also, the need to consciously counter the negative influence of the increasing violence around them, and its representation in the media, on the minds of children, and in its place promote a reflective engagement with more meaningful aspect of living an ethical and peaceful life. Education in the true sense should empower individuals to clarify their values; to enable them to take conscious and deliberate decisions, taking into considerations the consequences of their actions; to choose the way of peace rather than violence; to enable them to be makers of peace rather than consumers of peace.[1]

Strategies

Ethical development does not mean the imposition of do's and don'ts. Rather it calls for devising means and ways of helping children learn to make choices and decide what is right, what is kind, and what is best for the common good, keeping in view the broader implications for personnel and social values.

Children can understand almost everything they hear and see, but are often not able to reconcile contradictions between what is said and what is done. Even a minor disagreement at home can affect children very deeply. A state of permanent disaffection amongst the elders in the house or a disintegrating relationship between parents creates the kind of incalculable fear and depression that is often manifested as aggression a few years later in early youth. There is a need to bring parents and teachers together for more than only academic purposes. The responsibility of development of personal ethics does not rest solely with either parents or with the schools.

Ethical development follows different patterns characterising different age groups. During the primary years, children are still exploring their immediate environment and developing a consciousness of their own self. Their behaviour revolves around avoiding punishment and seeking rewards. They form notions of good and bad, right and wrong depending upon what is approved or disapproved by their elders. At this stage, what they see in the behaviour and action of adults prompts them to construct their own understanding of ethical behaviour.

As children grow older, their reasoning capabilities develop. However, they are still not mature enough to question assumptions and norms. Inspired by the need to impress others and validate their self-image as strong and capable individuals, they tend to violate rules. At this stage, facilitating reflection on the basis of rules and norms, restrictions, constraints, duties and obligations, etc., through discussion and dialogue, produces insight into the linkage between the collective good, the value of restraint, sacrifice, compassion, etc., which constitute the moral way of being.

Still later an abstract thinking is fully developed; individuals can make well-reasoned judgments about what constitutes ethical behaviour. This may lead to the acceptance and internalisation of ethical principles, which then can be sustained in the long run. Even in the absence of an external authority, ethically mature individuals behave in just and appropriate ways, and understand the basis of rules and, norms, and appreciate how these contribute to overall peace and order in society.

Our earliest and best teachers found stories and anecdotes the best way to get across an important spiritual teaching or social message. Along with this is the universal fact that every child, no matter how dull or uninspired his home life, has something to say, some insight to contribute to a class discussion. The teacher needs to draw out the children, gain their confidence, and avoid using threatening language or hostile body language.

Teaching values has often meant exhortations about desirable behaviour. It has also meant the suppression and denial of "improper" and "unacceptable" feelings and desires. This often leads children to hide their own real feelings, desires, thoughts and convictions and simply pay lip service to moral values and ideals, without making any commitment. Hence the need to move away from mere talk, to a meaningful discussion of experiences and reflections, eschewing a simplistic approach to moral behaviour, and instead exploring and understanding complex motivations and ethical dilemmas associated with human behaviour and actions.

Teacher should make deliberate attempts to infuse and reinforce the importance of peace related values that are commensurate with the textual material taught in school and developmental stages of children. For example, teachers can take advantage of the hidden components in a lesson by using appropriate strategies to awaken positive feelings, identifying experiences worth reflecting and, exploring, discovering, constructing, understanding peace-related values. Strategies like questions, stories, anecdotes, games, experiments, discussions, dialogues, clarification of values, examples, analogies, metaphors, role playing and simulation are helpful in promoting peace through teaching - learning. The teaching and practice of ethics go from the personal sphere to social and community-oriented thinking and then link up with global perspectives. A teacher who is oriented to the perspective of peace can introduce such opportunities for reflecting at these scales, and identifying the inter-linkages between them. Teacher education programmes should consider introducing peace education as an optional subject of study.[2]

1.3 (e) Position Paper - National Focus Group on Education for Peace (NCERT)

An expert committee was formed to consider in detail a programme for peace education based on NCF 2005. The position paper says –

Teacher education programmes need to prepare teachers as peace makers and peace builders through pre-service and in-service programmes. The following suggestions have been formulated for modifying teacher education programmes to that end.

Action Point

- A separate compulsory paper on 'Education for Peace' to be included in the foundation course of pre-service teacher education programmes.
- If this is not possible, peace concerns, attitudes and values may be incorporated into foundation papers.
- Student teachers may be given hands on practice, through internship, school experience programmes, and community work, etc., in the use of various conflict resolution techniques and textbook analysis and positive interpretation of content, etc.
- Cooperative learning techniques may form essential components of internship programme of pre-service teacher education programmes. A few lessons utilising these techniques may be made compulsory for all candidates.

- Regular in-service teacher training programmes, on content and pedagogy, of teachers and teacher educators may be organised separately on a regular basis.[3]

1.3 (f) National Curriculum Framework for Teacher Education (NCTE) and Peace Education

However, the teacher education curriculum framework of 1978, 1988 and 1998 emphasised the role of teachers as catalysts in the process of promoting social sensitivity, tolerance, co-operation, democratic and secular values, national integration, international understanding, etc. through inclusion of relevant themes in the 'Foundation Course' and 'School Experience' programmes. However, the existing realities and growing faith in violence among the teachers themselves in the form of corporal punishment given to students, caste and/or gender discrimination, religious prejudice, etc. indicate that teacher education programmes have not succeeded in equipping would be teachers with humane qualities essential for promoting a culture of peace in schools. Therefore, barring a few exceptions, teachers have ceased to be role models for vis-a-vis the students. Hence, it is essential to reconsider teacher education programme in order to equip teachers both through pre-service and in-service education for peace education.[4]

1.3 (g) NCF for Teacher Education 2009 (NCTE)

National curriculum framework (2009) for teacher education published by NCTE New Delhi in dosed the proposal on peace education in the framework of national curriculum framework of 2005 of NCERT. The NCF for teacher education 2009 says "peace provides an integrating principle for the value orientation of education. Education for peace is education for life, not merely training for livelihood. For equipping individuals with the values, skills and attitudes, they need to be wholesome persons who live in harmony with themselves and others and are responsible citizens is the goal of education for peace".[5]

The NCF of teacher education (2009) further says, "Peace education promotes peace values – democratic way of life, equality, justice, liberty, fraternity, secularism and zeal for social reconstruction.[6]

In this way what we need today is an education for developing peace culture that is capable of saving mankind from the present predicament. Such an education involves the spiritual development of man and the enhancement of his value as an individual and prepares the young people to understand the time in which they live. At school we must construct an environment in which children can be actively engaged in learning.

1.4 Meaning of Peace Education

Peace education in the Learning the way of peace (UNESCO) refers to "the process of promoting the knowledge, skills, attitudes and values needed to bring about behaviour changes that will enable children, youth and adults to prevent conflict and violence, both overt and structural; to resolve conflict peacefully; and to create the conditions conducive to peace, whether at an intrapersonal, intergroup, national or international level." [7]

1.5 Some Definitions of Peace Education

Peace education could be defined in many ways. There is no universally accepted definition as such.

A peace education is an attempt to respond to problems of conflict and violence on scales ranging from the global and national to the local and personal. It is about exploring ways of creating more just and sustainable futures. - R.D. Laing (1978)[8]

Peace education is holistic. It embraces the physical, emotional, intellectual, and social growth of children within a framework deeply rooted in traditional human values. It is based on philosophy that teaches love, compassion, trust, fairness, co-operation and reverence for the human family and all life on our beautiful planet. - Fran Schmidt and Alice Friedman (1988) [9]

Peace education is skill building. It empowers children to join creative and nondestructive ways to settle conflict and to live in harmony with themselves, others, and their world . . . Peace building is the task of every human being and the challenge of the human family. -Fran Schmidt and Alice Friedman (1988) [10]

1.6 Aims of Peace Education

- To help students understand some of the complex processes leading to violence and conflict at the individual, group, national and global levels, and be aware of some of the ways in which these conflicts may be resolved.
- To encourage attitudes that lead to a preference for constructive and nonviolent resolution of conflict.
- To assist students in developing the personal and social skills necessary to live in harmony with others and to behave in positive and caring ways that respect the basic human rights.
- To develop human learning communities in which students and teachers are encouraged to work together cooperatively to understand and find resolutions to significant problems.[11]

1.7 Peace Education: An Essential Component of Quality Basic Education

Peace education is an integral part of the UNICEF vision of quality basic education. The 1990 World Declaration on Education for All (the Jomtien Declaration) clearly states that basic learning needs comprise not only essential tools such as literacy and numeracy, but also the knowledge, skills, attitudes and values required to live and work with dignity and to participate in development. It further states that the satisfaction of those needs implies a responsibility to promote social justice, acceptance of differences, and peace (Inter-Agency Commission, WCEFA, 1990).

Basic education is a process that encompasses the knowledge, skills, attitudes and values needed to live peacefully in an interdependent world. 'The Future Global Agenda for Children – Imperatives for the Twenty-First Century' (UNICEF 1999, E/ICEF/1999/10) makes a commitment to "... ensure that education and learning processes help to form both human capital for economic growth and social capital for tolerance, respect for others and the right of each individual to participate with equality within family, community and economic life; ... and to challenge the culture of violence that threatens to destroy family and community life in so many countries."[12]

1.8 Role of Schools in Promoting Peace Education

The basic concepts embedded in the definitions of peace education are that peace education is a remedial measure to protect children from falling into the web of violence prevalent in the society. It aims at the total development of the child. It tries to inculcate higher human and social values in the mind of the child. In essence, it attempts to develop a set of behavioural skills necessary for peaceful living and peace-building from which the whole humanity will be benefited.

In fact, two out of the four pillars of education suggested by the Delor's report, namely, learning to live together and learning to be, are related to peaceful living. So, it is essential to integrate peaceful attitudes, values, and skills into the teaching and learning process in school and to make it a part of the total curriculum. Certain countries and institutes have it in the form of subjects such as Values Education, (Malaysia and Philippines), Citizenship Education (USA), Education for Mutual Understanding (Ireland) and Developmental Education (UNICEF). Apart from such subjects, it can be integrated into the formal curriculum and co-curriculum of schools. Through applying peace education and creating a peace culture, it has been observed that schools can have the following benefits:

- Develop a more humanistic management approach.
- Improve human relations between teacher-student, teacher-teacher, student-student, etc.
- Help develop good attitudes in the students and teachers, e.g., co-operation, mutual respect.
- Help healthy emotional development in students.
- Facilitate socialisation through participation in interactive and co-operative learning activities.

- Improve students' discipline and moral behaviour.
- Develop the creativity both in students and teachers.
- Improve the standard of teaching and learning.[13]

1.9 Role of Teachers in Promoting Peace Education

- The teacher must understand that multicultural, multiethnic, and multireligious problems in society are not to be dealt with in isolation in bits and pieces of a good peace education programme but, being interconnected with all other problems of peace and violence, are addressed in the whole programme. For example, developing qualities such as compassion and service to others can help reduce racial, religious, or other prejudices, but students of all backgrounds must take part in the programme.
- The teacher must be cognizant and wholly supportive of the basic nature and aims of peace education. According to Dale Hudson, "...education that actualizes (people's) potentialities in helping them learns how to make peace with themselves and with others, to live in harmony and unity with self, humankind and nature." The principles upon which this statement rests include: 1. The cardinal prerequisite for world peace is the unity of humankind. 2. World order can be founded only on the consciousness of the oneness of humankind. It follows that, in this view, the teacher of peace education in an apparently diverse society must keep certain basic aims in mind: the achievement of a unified, peaceful society both globally and within the nation, where world citizenship is fostered and "unity in diversity" is recognised and practiced.
- The teacher should constantly keep in mind that the attainment of any aim is conditioned upon knowledge, volition, and action. Unless these three are forthcoming, nothing will be accomplished. The power needed to accomplish a peaceful world is the unification of humankind. To this end, the teacher must use his will-power. In the words of Sarvepalli Radhakrishnan, we should "... will peace with our whole body and soul, our feelings and instincts, our flesh and its

affections." Then we should act intelligently to reduce intercultural, interethnic, and inter-religious violence, bringing a greater degree of unity and harmony in society. To accomplish this, the teacher should develop qualities such as tolerance, respect of and appreciation of others, being fair and open-minded, and being able and willing to consider other points of view looking beyond his or her own self-interest. In other words, the teacher must be sincerely attempting to be free of prejudice.

- When a teacher becomes deeply and regularly involved in teaching peace education, it gives him an opportunity to take a long, deep look at his or her values and beliefs. In order to be a model for the students, the teacher has the opportunity of transformation and could modify his inner self. This modification would help the students to understand who is a peaceful person and a peacemaker. Thus, the teacher will have a powerful, positive influence on hundreds and thousands of children and youth.
- Teachers must cope with prejudices, conflicts, and violence in an increasingly diverse society by starting with themselves. Firstly, the teacher must develop his own emotional intelligence. People with high EQ know and manage their own emotional life well and understand and deal effectively with the feelings of others. They are skillful in relationships.

1.10 Justification of the Present Study

The present world is turning into a global village; every citizen of the world wants this global village to be a place of peace based on the principle of freedom, equality and fraternity. This global village is also a place with plural democratic society. The idea of global village is very attractive but it is facing many serious social, political and economical imbalances. Value crisis is very deep-rooted in the present world. The whole world is divided into racial, religious, caste, class and ethnic groups. The arms race and nuclear technology is also posing a serious threat to human survival. Terrorism, violence, racial superiority and intolerance are eroding basic human values.

The global village should change its perspectives from narrow nationalism to universalism, from ethnic and cultural prejudice to tolerance, understanding and pluralism. There is an urgent need to create a culture of nonviolence and tolerance in all walks of life, which may help in creating a peaceful and affectionate society. The need to make the present world a peaceful global village is being felt by educationists and they are of the view that the most effective and permanent instrument to achieve the above objective is the instrument of education.

If one wants to make education an instrument for achieving peace and harmony in the present world, it is possible only through developing awareness for peace education among the teachers. Teacher's colleges are the place where we are preparing the prospective teachers. These prospective teachers can make the students aware of peaceful activities and enlightened behaviour. In this way, one can say that the present research work is need-based and very useful for promoting peace and harmony in the minds of our future citizens.

1.11 Statement of the Research Problem

The title of the present research work is "Developing awareness for the teaching of peace education among prospective teachers."

1.12 Specific Objectives of the Research

I. To find out the awareness about peace education among the prospective teachers.

II. To find out the problematic areas (contents in teaching package) through pre test related with peace education among prospective teachers.

III. Prepare a teaching package for the teaching of peace education for prospective teachers.

IV. To teach the prospective teachers about peace education through the package.

V. To find out the impact of teaching package among the prospective teachers (through post test).

VI. To find out the opinion of the principals (teachers college) and experts about developing awareness of teaching of peace education among the prospective teachers.

1.13 Technical Terms

In this research the following technical terms are being used –

Awareness

In this research awareness means:

(a) Understanding the concept of peace education.

(b) Appreciation for teaching of peace education.

Teaching of Peace Education

In this research teaching of peace education means teaching through the teaching package which will consist of the following points:

(a) Knowledge and understanding of meaning and concept of peace education.

(b) Understanding the spirit of peace education.

(c) Application of the concept and components of peace education.

Prospective Teachers

Here, prospective teachers mean all the regular B.Ed. students for one academic session of teachers college.

1.14 Review of Related Literature

A detailed review of related literature was carried out by the researcher from libraries and net surfing.

1.15 Selection of Method and Design

Looking at the nature of present research work, experimental method was used by the researcher. For his investigation pre-test, post-test experimental design was used.

1.16 Variables

In the present study teaching package prepared by the researcher was taken as an Independent Variable (I.V.) while awareness for the teaching of peace education was considered as Dependent Variable (D.V.).

1.17 Hypothesis

In this study researcher used the null hypotheses for finding the effectiveness of teaching package of peace education.

1.18 Selection of Sample

The sample was selected on the basis of purposive and random sampling.

1.19 Tools

Researcher used self made pre-and post-test, teaching package and semi-structured interview schedule as experimental tools.

1.20 Procedure

To carry out the investigation, the researcher administered the pre-test on subjects of all the groups. After the pre-experimental measurement the subjects of experimental group were taught peace education through teaching package for a period of three weeks and the students of control group were indulged in their normal activities for the same span of time. To measure the effectiveness of teaching package post-test was administered on the subjects of experimental as well as control group.

1.21 Statistical Design

To compare the effect of various independent variables (IV's) on the subjects of both groups the researcher used inter and intra group comparison.

1.22 Analysis and Interpretation of the Data

After analysis and interpretation of data final conclusion were drawn.

1.23 Delimitation

The present research study is confined to the two hundred women B.Ed. trainees of two teachers college of Rajasthan state.

1.24 Conclusion

The purpose of the first chapter is to introduce development, meaning, definitions and aims of peace education. It also describes the role of schools and teachers in promoting peace education. The chapter states the justification of the present study, statement of the research problem, specific objectives of the research, technical terms and delimitation of the present research. It also describes in brief the method and design, sample, tests and tools and statistical design of the study.

References

1. NCERT (2005), National Curriculum Framework for School Education, NCERT, New Delhi.
2. *Ibid.*
3. NCERT (2006), Position Paper of the National Focus Group on Peace Education, NCERT, New Delhi.
4. *Ibid.*
5. National Curriculum Framework for Teacher Education (2009), NCTE, New Delhi.
6. *Ibid.*
7. Fountain, S. (1999), Peace Education in UNICEF, Working Paper, Education Section, Programme Division, UNICEF, New York.
8. Balasooriya, A.S. (2001), Learning the Way of Peace: A Teachers' Guide to Peace Education, United Nations Educational, Scientific and Cultural Organisation, New Delhi.

9. *Ibid.*

10. *Ibid.*

11. Bagchi, J.P. and Teckchandani V. (2005), Values Education, University Book House Pvt. Limited, Jaipur.

12. Fountain, S. (1999), Peace Education in UNICEF, Working Paper, Education Section, Programme Division, UNICEF, New York.

13. Balasooriya, A.S. 2001, Learning the Way of Peace: A Teachers' Guide to Peace Education, United Nations Educational, Scientific and Cultural Organisation, New Delhi.

2

Review of the Related Literature

First chapter purported to give a synoptic view of the study as such. The present chapter has been designed to give a brief review of the researches done in the field.

2.1 Introduction

Basic and fundamental researches have been carried out in education since long. Most of these studies are confined to theoretical investigations only but it cannot be denied that they have added a lot to the innovations and improvement of our measure of knowledge. But the recent trend in the field of education is to investigate into the existing means to solve the problem faced by the people working in that field. Before embarking on a new area of research in any field, an adequate survey of related literature has been rightly considered as an important and inevitable pre-requisite to proper planning and execution of any scientific research.

The review of related literature is very difficult task indeed. In every kind of scientific research whether it is in the field of physical sciences or in that of the social sciences the related literature is the first step of utmost importance.

The study of the related literature pertaining to the problem is the first base of the investigation. By studying the related literature the researcher knows how much work has been done on the problem so far. The investigator will then know and judge from where he has to start and what should be his design and procedure of the study.

2.2 Meaning of Review of Related Literature

The task of review of related literature is highly creative and tedious because researcher has to synthesise the available knowledge of the field in a unique way to provide the rationale for his study.

"The competent physician must keep abreast of the latest discoveries in the field of medicine. Obviously the careful student of education, the research worker and the investigator should become familiar with location and use of sources of educational information."[1]

"The literature in any field forms the foundation upon which all future work will be built. If we fail to build the foundation of knowledge provided by the review of literature our work is likely to be shallow and naive and will often duplicate work that has already been done better by someone else."[2]

"A survey of related literature is necessary for proper planning, execution and right concept of the problem and its solution. It provides guiding hypothesis, suggestive method of investigation and comparative data for interpretative purposes."[3]

Good, Barr and Scates have the following views:

(a) The study of the related literature saves the researcher from duplication and repetition.

(b) The study of the related literature helps in organising the ideas, information of hypothesis and planning the design.

(c) It helps the researcher in developing his/her knowledge.

(d) It develops insight in the investigator.

(e) The study of earlier researches helps in determining new problems.[4]

Borg says, "The review of the literature in educational

research provides one with means of getting the frontier in a particular field of knowledge".[5]

That is, it enables a researcher to locate, read and evaluate the related work previously done, to gain accurate knowledge of the completed aspects of the research problem in hand and to get benefit from similar studies. Review of related literature also gives a clear idea for procedure of data collection, analysis and interpretation of data. It also suggests pattern for writing the conclusion and areas for further researches. All this demands hard labour, patience, and also skill. John W. Best has very aptly said that "the searching and reviewing of the related material is a time-consuming but fruitful phase of the graduate programme. A familiarity with the literature of any problem area helps the student discover what is already known, what other have attempted to find out, what methods of attack have been promising and disappointing and what problems remain to be solved".[6]

In a survey, the review of the literature serves a variety of background functions preparatory to actual collection of data. In this research approach, the literature is reviewed to create the contest from the past for the new study to be conducted with new subjects and newly gathered data.

Reviewing the literature has two phases. The first phase includes identifying all the relevant published material in the problem area and reading that part of it with which we are not thoroughly familiar, we develop the foundation of idea and results on which our own study will be built.

The second phase of the review of related literature involves writing this foundation of ideas into a section of the research report. This section is for the joint benefit of the researchers and readers. For the researcher, it establishes the background in the field.

2.3 Need of Review of Related Literature

1. One of the early steps in planning a research work is to review research done previously in the particular area of interest

and relevant area, quantitative and qualitative analysis of this research usually gives the worker an indication of the direction.

2. It is very essential for every investigator to be up-to-date in his information about the literature, related to his own problem already done by others. It is considered to be the most important pre-requisite to actual planning and conducting the study.
3. Avoids the replication of the study of findings to take an advantage from similar or related literature as regards, to methodology, techniques of data collection, procedure adopted and conclusion drawn. One can justify ones endeavour in the field.
4. It provides a source of problem of study. An analogy may be drawn for identifying and selecting the problem of research. The researcher formulates his/her hypotheses on the basis of review of literature. It also provides the rationale for the study. The results and findings of the study can also be discussed at length.

2.4 Purpose of Review of Literature

The review of the related literature serves the following purposes in conducting research work:

1. It provides theories, ideas, and explanations of hypothesis which may prove useful in the formulation of new problem.
2. It indicates whether the evidence already available solves the problem adequately without requiring further investigation. It avoids the replication.
3. It provides the sources for hypotheses. The researcher can formulate research hypotheses on the basis of available studies.
4. It suggests methods, procedure, sources of data and statistical techniques appropriate to the solution of the problem.
5. It locates comparative data and is found useful in the interpretation and discussion of results. The conclusions

drawn in the related studies may be significantly compared and may be used as the subject for the findings of the study.

6. It helps in developing expertise and general scholarship of the investigator in the area investigated.
7. It contributes towards the accurate knowledge of the evidence or literature in ones area of activity. This knowledge is an asset ever afterwards whether one is employed in an institution of higher learning or a research organisation.

In order to have a clear understanding of the work done in the field of peace education, the investigator tried to find the studies done in the field. The related literature found during survey work of libraries and net surfing has been divided in two sections. The categorisation of the reviewed work is given below:

(a) Articles related to subject of the study.

(b) Researches done in the related field.

2.5 Review of Related Literature

(a) Articles related to subject of the study

1. Monisha Bajaj[7] (2010) in her article "Conjectures on peace education and Gandhian studies: method, institutional development and globalisation" examined the similarities and differences in the field of Gandhian studies and peace education through an exploration of their content, institutional development, and globalisation since the mid-twentieth century. The methods utilised include document review of syllabi and course descriptions in Gandhian studies and peace education, as well as interviews with individuals taken in both fields. Through an examination of the history, emergence and core concepts in each field, this article argues that both fields have the potential to offer each other important lessons based in their own unique trajectories. Specifically, it was found that educational movements and structural analysis of power and inequality that are often integral to them, can inform peace education by diversifying the voices deemed canonical in the field. Similarly, Gandhian studies, in responding to the unique

dilemma of expanding resources and institutionalisation amidst decreasing student demand, may do well to broaden its foci and further integrate contemporary social issues related to peace and social justice.

2. The study by Renat Shaykhutdinov[8] (2010) entitled "Give peace a chance: Non-violent protest and the creation of territorial autonomy arrangements" examines factors that predict the formation of territorial autonomy arrangements for regionally concentrated ethnic communities. Territorial autonomies are institutional arrangements that allow ethnic groups to express their distinct identities while keeping the borders of host states intact. Although an extensive literature has investigated the capacity of autonomy arrangements to manage interethnic disputes, little research has addressed the precise origins of these institutions. The existing literature considers violent tactics as a primary factor that enables ethnic collectivities to attain territorial autonomy. In this study, the reasoning from the literature is juxtaposed with the arguments developed in the research on nonviolent opposition. Nonviolent movements enjoy moral advantage vis-à-vis violent groups. Moreover, peaceful tactics have the advantage of garnering attention for the concerns of ethnic groups without the liability of provoking the animosity or distrust created by violent conflict. Based on the analysis of a dataset representing 168 ethnic groups across 87 states from 1945 to 2000, it is found that the peaceful tactics groups employ when seeking greater self-rule is the single strongest predictor of the formation of autonomy arrangements. In particular, this study concludes that groups that rely on peaceful tactics, such as protests and strikes, and demand territorial autonomy, as opposed to an outright independence, have a greater potential to achieve territorial autonomy in comparison to those groups making extreme demands through the use of violence.

3. The study by Yaacov Boaz Yablon[9] (2009) entitled "Gender differences in peace education programmes, Gender and Education" aimed to reveal gender differences regarding peace and peace pedagogy. Peace education programmes have become part of the school curriculum all over the world, as a

way to enhance positive relationships between conflict groups. Although gender differences are being taken into account when planning various educational programmes, this is usually not the case with peace education. In this study one hundred and eighty Israeli Jewish and Arab high school students participated in a peace contact education programme. Gender and group differences were examined both before and after participation in the programme. The findings revealed that the Jewish and Arab female youths were more dovish than the males both before and after participating in the programme, and gained more from the encounters. Implications for conflict resolution and peace pedagogy are discussed.

4. The qualitative study by Pamela Bolotin Joseph and Leslie Smith Duss [10] (2009) entitled "Teaching a pedagogy of peace: a study of peace educators in United States schools in the aftermath of September 11" is based on in-depth semi-structured interviews, depicts practices of seven peace educators in public elementary and secondary classrooms in the United States during the time of the terrorist attacks on 11 September 2001 through the US engagement in war in Afghanistan and Iraq. Focusing on individual perceptions of practice and classroom experiences, the participants described how, despite teaching at a time in which terrorism and war had become national preoccupations, they taught pedagogy of peace that included recognition and rejection of violence, understanding of differences through dialogue, critical awareness of injustice and social justice, and imaginative understanding of peace. The study discloses a multitude of examples of both peacemaking and peace building in their teaching and development of classroom cultures but a lack of emphasis on anti-war curriculum. It also reveals the teachers' motivations for teaching peace education, theoretical influences on their practice, their identities as activists and examples of their curriculum leadership.

5. The article by Noam Schimmel[11] (2009), Towards a Sustainable and Holistic Model of Peace Education: a Critique of Conventional Modes of Peace Education Through Dialogue in Israel, (2009) entitled "Towards a sustainable and holistic

model of peace education: a critique of conventional modes of peace education through dialogue in Israel", explores ways of improving peace education, placing emphasis on peace education programmes in Israel that use dialogue to foster mutual understanding and respect. This article offers a critical assessment of contemporary Israeli peace education initiatives, emphasising that current peace education programmes in Israel have failed to significantly improve social attitudes between Arabs and Jews. Critiques of contemporary forms of peace education focus on their psychological and social contexts, and the ways in which the framing of peace education has substantive impacts on the likelihood of its success and its sustainability. Emphasis is placed on the importance of incorporating affective rather than primarily cognitive models for promoting coexistence; the importance of pursuing long-term peace education programming rather than the predominant short-term 'encounter group' model; and the need for a comprehensive social and political approach to peace education that extends beyond schools and embraces society as a whole.

6. Candice C. Carter[12] (2008) in his article entitled "Voluntary standards for peace education", suggests that peace education is comprehensive. It encompasses instruction by all members of a school. These standards, which were recommended by researchers and practitioners from many areas of the world, prescribe comprehensive and simultaneous instruction with informal as well as formal curriculum. Although the voluntary standards are a response to new liberal policies in the field of education, they were born of enduring concepts along with research on educational practice and peace development. As the international community and its various schools grapple with several types of violence, comprehensive peace education provides student preparation for responsible stewardship through an enacted vision of a better world. In this article author included recommendations for providing such transformative education. The standards that embody those recommendations have been aids to instructors who implement peace education.

7. The article by H.B. Danesh[13] (2008) entitled "The Education for Peace integrative curriculum: concepts, contents and efficacy", presents the conceptual foundations of the Education for Peace (EFP) integrative curriculum, reviews its contents, and briefly describes its impact on students, teachers, staff and parents/guardians in Bosnia and Herzegovina. The curriculum was developed in 2000, first employed in six pilot schools and then implemented in 112 primary and secondary schools in Bosnia and Herzegovina as well as in a few schools in North America, thus far involving thousands of educators and tens of thousands of students. The curriculum is being published in nine volumes covering core aspects of peace education. This article reviews the curriculum's comprehensive and inclusive pedagogical approaches and unique conceptual formulation, which defines conflict as the absence of unity and unity as the main prerequisite for peace. The curriculum integrates insights from a wide range of disciplines on peace and education, including education, peace studies, conflict resolution, political science, law, religion, sociology, psychology and history. Within this integrative approach, each volume addresses one or more aspects of peace and peace education, drawing from the latest developments in the field and from lessons learned in the implementation of the EFP programme. The final part of the article includes several first-hand statements attesting the efficacy of the EFP programme.

8. Ole Henning Sommerfelt and Vidar Vambheim[14] (2008) in their article "The dream of the good'-a peace education project exploring the potential to educate for peace at an individual level", numerous educational efforts have been tried in order to address problems of conflicts and violence at various levels of society. These efforts have been effective to various degrees. This article investigates the effectiveness of the Swedish-based peace education project 'The dream of the good' (DODG), through its use of mind/body-oriented methods, to develop non-violent attitudes and behaviour (peacefulness) in individual students. This investigation is integrated into a wider discussion of whether didactic

programmes may be planned and implemented to effect such changes. The article first discusses assumptions related to the development of students' peacefulness, and how effective existing peace programmes are towards this end. Following a presentation of DODG, mechanisms of aggression and peaceful development are reviewed theoretically, with particular reference to mind/body-oriented methods, from the perspectives of behavioural science and Buddhist philosophy. Finally, empirical findings from an interview study of DODG and a small controlled follow-up study are presented.

9. The article by Ruth Firer[15] (2008) entitled "Virtual peace education, Journal of Peace Education", is based on the convictions that peace education is the basis for any sustainable non-violent relations between parties in a conflict, and that virtual peace education is almost the only feasible way to practise peace education in an open violent conflict as is the current Israeli/Palestinians one. Moreover, virtual peace education has an independent rationale that justifies its merits as an additional model of peace education, in a post-conflict process of healing and among parties in societies torn by rifts and problems. This article includes highlights of the Israeli peace education experience from the early twentieth century until the present stage that is characterised by virtual peace education. It contains a basic taxonomy of virtual learning and virtual peace education that is followed by offering the arguments for and against it as based on the observations of researchers and on concrete occurrences in Israeli/Palestinian experience. The article concludes with a reference to a case study of the higher education course 'From war culture to peace education' as elaborated by the author for ODISEAME - the European Middle East Virtual University, and a proposal to establish a virtual international peace school.

10. The research by Yaacov Boaz Yablon[16] (2007), entitled "Cognitive rather than emotional modification in peace education programmes: advantages and limitations", seeks to reveal the force driving processes that lead to positive contact between conflict groups, and points to the importance of emotional modification. Acknowledging the centrality of

emotional modification, the present study points to the importance of defining the desired goals of contact interventions. Contact intervention programmes are being used as the main vehicle to enhance positive relationships between conflict groups. Current research aimed to reveal which of the emotional, cognitive, motivational or behavioural components of inter group relations were most enhanced in peace intervention programs for Israeli Jewish and Bedouin Arab high-school students in Israel. The findings indicate the cognitive realm as the most enhanced. These findings raise the question of the relevance of emotional modification in regions of persistent conflict, and suggests that intervention methods and desired outcomes must be closely linked. Finally, implications for moral education are discussed.

11. Anita L. Wenden[17] (2007) in her article entitled " Educating for a critically literate civil society: incorporating the linguistic perspective into peace education", is of the view that despite the multifaceted role language plays in promoting direct and indirect violence, activities that would develop the linguistic knowledge and critical language skills for understanding how discourse shapes individual and group beliefs and prompts social action are conspicuously absent from peace education. This article aims to address this absence. It will present a framework for promoting critical language awareness, discuss its relevance to the preparation of critically literate citizens and suggests ways of incorporating it into programmes and curricula that educate for peace.

12. David W. Johnson and Roger T. Johnson[18] (2006) in his article entitled "Peace education for consensual peace: the essential role of conflict resolution", claims that peace education is a key for establishing and maintaining a consensual peace. Creating an effective peace education program involves five steps. First, a public education system must be established with compulsory attendance; all children and youth should attend so that students from the previously conflicting groups interact and have the opportunity to build positive relationships with each other. Second, a sense of mutuality and common fate needs to be established that highlights mutual goals, the

'just' distribution of benefits from achieving the goals, and a common identity. In schools, this is primarily done through the use of cooperative learning. Third, students should be taught the constructive controversy procedure to ensure that they know how to make difficult decisions and engage in political discourse. Fourth, students should be taught how to engage in integrative negotiations and peer mediation to resolve their conflicts with each other constructively. Finally, civic values should be inculcated that focus students on the long-term common good of society.

13. The paper by H.B. Danesh[19] (2006) entitled "Towards an integrative theory of peace education", proposes the integrative theory of peace (ITP) and briefly outlines the education for peace curriculum (EFP) developed on the basis of this theory. ITP is based on the concept that peace is, at once, a psychological, social, political, ethical and spiritual state with its expressions in intrapersonal, interpersonal, inter group, international, and global areas of human life. The theory holds that all human states of being, including peace, are shaped by our worldview - our view of reality, human nature, purpose of life and human relationships. Four prerequisites for effective peace education - unity - based worldview, culture of healing, culture of peace and peace-oriented curriculum - are discussed. The paper supports the conceptual elements of the ITP by drawing from the existing body of research on peace education and the EFP experience in Bosnia and Herzegovina (BiH) where, since 2000, some 112 BiH schools with almost 80,000 students, along with their parents and teachers, have begun to systematically introduce the principles and practices of EFP into the curriculum and operation of their respective schools.

14. Johnson, David W. and Johnson, Roger T.[20] (2005) in their article "Essential Components of Peace Education", writes that peace education is a key for establishing a consensual peace and maintaining it over time. There are five essential elements in building a lasting peace through education. First, a public education system must be established with compulsory

attendance for all children and youth. It will motivate students from previously conflicting groups, bringing an interaction with one another and giving them an opportunity to build positive relationships with one another. Second, a sense of mutuality and common fate needs to be established that highlights mutual goals, the just distribution of benefits from achieving the goals, and a common identity. In schools, this is primarily done through the use of cooperative learning. Third, students must be taught the constructive controversy procedure to ensure that they know how to make difficult decisions and engage in political discourse. Fourth, students must be taught how to engage in integrative negotiations and peer mediation to resolve their conflicts with each other constructively. Finally, civic values must be inculcated that focus students on the long-term common good of society.

15. According to Kupermintz, Haggai and Salomon Gavriel[21] (2005) in the article entitled "Lessons to Be Learned From Research on Peace Education in the Context of Intractable Conflict", writes that recent research on peace education entails important practical lessons about educational work in regions of intractable conflict. Peace education in this context must deal with collective narratives and deeply rooted historical memories and societal beliefs. Research findings from a series of studies with Israeli and Palestinian students and teachers demonstrate the challenges of attaining durable and worthwhile effects through educational activities: short-term benefits may erode over time, ongoing violence and hostility may block attempts to understand the opponent's perspective, and power and status asymmetries may dictate incompatible agendas or prohibit a mutual common ground for constructive interaction. At the same time, these studies offer several promising directions to enhance the potential of carefully designed peace education programmes. Such programmes are likely to foster participants' ability to acknowledge the adversary's collective narrative, engage in constructive negotiations over issues of national identity, and express a less monolithic outlook of the conflict.

16. The paper by Simon Harris, Nick Lewer[22] (2005) entitled "Post-graduate peace education in Sri Lanka", summarises the rationale, development, content, and delivery of a Post Graduate Diploma in Conflict Resolution and Peace Preparedness in Sri Lanka, a country that has experienced a violent and protracted social conflict over the last 25 years. It also describes the methodology which is being used to measure the peace impact of the programme. Difficulties encountered and lessons learned are discussed, and some early indicators of the effectiveness of the programmes were evaluated. It is clear that the impact of such a programme cannot be fully measured in a short term, since peace education should be seen as a process whereby knowledge and skills gained can be both utilised in the short term and reflected upon in the long term.
17. The paper by Claire McGlynn[23] (2004) entitled "Education for peace in integrated schools: a priority for Northern Ireland?", argues that a vital purpose of education in Northern Ireland should be peace building and the promotion of social cohesion. In particular, the paper looks at the lessons that can be learned from integrated education by societies moving out of conflict. As a part of a larger study of the impact of integrated (mixed Catholic and Protestant) education, former and current Principals of the two longest established post-primary (for children aged 11-18) integrated colleges were questioned about the policies and practice employed by their schools with regards to promoting respect for diversity, dealing with cultural symbols and affirming or challenging identity. The potential of integrated education to promote tolerance and understanding is discussed. This paper concludes that the needs of children and society for reconciliation through integrated schooling should perhaps take preference over the rights of parents to segregated education.
18. Gavriel Salomon[24] (2004) in his article entitled "Does Peace Education Make a Difference in the Context of an Intractable Conflict?", reveals that peace education in regions of intractable conflict faces a number of severe challenges, such

as conflicting collective narratives, shared histories and beliefs, grave inequalities, excessive emotionality, and unsupportive social climates. It shows that the chances of success for peace education programmes are rather slim. A series of quasi-experimental studies carried out with Israeli-Jewish and Palestinian youngsters revealed that despite the ongoing violence, participation in various programmes yields positive attitudinal, perceptual, and relational changes, for example, more positive views of "peace", better ability to see the other side's perspective, and greater willingness for contact. These changes depend on participants' initial political views, and thus, as found in one study, play an attitude-reinforcing function, but, as found in another study, prevent the worsening of perceptions of and attribution to the other side, thereby serving in a preventive capacity.

19. The paper by Brantmeier, Edward J [25] (2003) entitled "Peace Pedagogy: Exposing and Integrating Peace Education in Teacher Education", discusses peace education, as "the transmission of knowledge about the requirements of the obstacles to and possibilities for achieving and maintaining peace, training in skills for interpreting the knowledge, and development of reflective and participatory capacities for applying the knowledge to overcome problems and achieving possibilities." The paper asserts that peace education needs exposure and further integration into teacher education discourse and practice. It begins defining peace education, explaining how the purposes and goals of peace education already align with peace theory, and suggesting how a move from implicit to explicit peace education may strengthen the overall momentum of peace pedagogy in building a culture of peace. The paper also surveys the scholarly literature pertaining to the integration of peace education into teacher education (noting that it has been excluded from mainstream teacher education rhetoric), and it reviews how peace education has been and can be further integrated into teacher education rhetoric and practice. It concludes by discussing approaches to peace education, a semantic field for peace education, and building a culture of peace through teacher education.

20. In an educational report by Bjerstedt, Ake[26] (2003) entitled "Developing Preparedness for Peace: Objectives, Methods, Difficulties and Possibilities in Peace-Related Education", the educators at the Malmo School of Education (Sweden) have carried out a series of studies within the area of school and peace. As an informal umbrella heading for the project group conducting such studies the term "Preparedness for Peace" has been used. The overriding aim of the group's work has been to increase knowledge (in a broad sense) about hindrances and possibilities in the schools work with global survival issues. This overview report collects notes about the work of the project group and the process they have been involved in. The report also presents some of the group's views on possible and fruitful ways of dealing with conflict and peace education that have resulted from the group's work (the product). It is divided into nine sections:

    (1) Introduction; (2) What is Preparedness for Peace? A Discussion about the Ambitions and Specific Objectives of Peace Education; (3) What Can We Do in School to Promote Preparedness for Peace? (4) Some "Difficulties" with Peace Education; (5) Peace Education and Teacher Training; (6) Developing Students' Materials and Teachers' Manuals; (7) Continued Work: Need for Flexible Fact-Finding"; (8) Issues for Thought and Dialogue; and (9) Postscriptum. These nine sections successfully deal with conflict and peace education.

21. The study by Yaacov B. Yablon and Yaacov J. Katz[27] (2001) entitled "Internet-Based Group Relations: A High School Peace Education Project in Israel", describes how the Internet-based group communications was used as the major strategy to promote the societal values of understanding, equality, tolerance and peace between Israeli Jewish and Bedouin high school students. The Internet-based communications project formed the backbone of a project designed to confront one of the major conflicts in Israeli society, which focuses on the Jewish-Arab axis. Israeli Jews and Arabs are wary of each other and latent hostility permeates the atmosphere between the two societal groups and is directly related to the Israeli-

Arab conflict. In the project the societal values of understanding, equality, tolerance and peace were intensely promoted through the medium of three different complementary educational strategies. Students participated in workshops conducted by experts trained in the art of mediation and bridge building, and in two day-long face-to-face meetings. The major strategy was an Internet-based weekly chat-room and e-mail session which lasted for the full length of the project. All three strategies were specially designed to promote understanding, equality, tolerance and peace between Jewish and Bedouin Arab students. The results of the project indicate that Jewish students adopted more favourable attitudes toward Bedouins and those Bedouin students' attitudes towards Jewish students remained positive throughout the duration of the project. The prognosis for long-term change and cooperation between the Jewish and Bedouin students who participated in the project is also discussed.

(b) Researches done in the related field

1. Bogart, Louise Berry, 2000, "A qualitative study of classroom culture in two elementary environments in which teachers who identify themselves as peace educators are implementing peace education practices with first grade children" Ph.D., University of Hawaii at Manoa.

   Objective of the study:

   The objective was to learn about the ways in which teachers educated children for positive peace. It explored factors that influenced teacher commitment to peace education.

   Method: Case study method.

   Tool: Questionnaire, interview and observation.

   Sample: Teachers of Hawaiian Public schools and Roman Catholic Teachers.

   Result: Caring and cooperation offered assistance to the children in academic and social situations. The classroom was a safe place both emotionally and physically. Teachers shared power by giving children a voice in decisions that concerned them. Conflict resolution involved the use of problem solving skills including appropriate language. The data provide two portraits of how peace education might be approached in primary classrooms. Both concentrated on the quality of live experience rather than on introducing curriculum. The study showed that peace education can be cultivated by two different teachers in different settings and still produce similar results of positive, non-violent behaviour.

2. Brown,Warren Donald, 2000, "School Children's perception of conflict : A view from the urban inner-city", Ph.D., Nova Southeastern University.

   Objective of the study:

   To bring peaceful environment in schools and society by implementing conflict resolution programme.

   Method: Case study method.

   Tool: Questionnaire and Observation.

   Result: The implementation of conflict resolution programme in schools will play an important role in decreasing violence in teaching organisation.

3. Adenike Yesufu, 2000, "Education for a culture of peace in Nigeria : The role of a womens development NGO", Ph.D., University of Alberta Canada.

   Objective of the study:

   To study the contribution of women in building culture of peace.

   Method: Qualitative research method.

   Tool: Interview, Observation, Analysis of relevant documents.

Result:

1. The main focus of WLDC (Women law development centre) Programme was on the development of women

but this kind of organised teaching work is very much relevant in building the culture of peace.

2. WLDC has awakened women towards their social and economic problems.
3. The training strategies reflect those process and values which are similar to culture of peace.
4. WLDC adopted non-violence, conflict resolution and values to establish peaceful brotherhood.
5. Positive coordination was found between women NGO and culture of peace and values.

4. Hursh, Lydia Heidi, 2001, "A peace education study : Perceptation of U.S. adolescent women in international peace building camp", Ph.D., University of Denevar.

Objectives of the study:

1. To describe the peace building process in camp and study the effect of its curriculum on ten American participants.
2. To know the expected areas of changes in three different fields on participants
   (a) Participants perception on their self-development.
   (b) Perception of participants' cultural recognition.
   (c) Change in participants' opinion for Israelians and Palestinean.

Method: Survey Method.

Tool: Observation, Focus group interview and journals analysis.

Result:

(a) American as a third party in camp played an important role for making emotional encouragement in co-operation of Isrealians and Philistines struggle.

(b) Americans tried to make close relationship with middle east participants which helped them to understand conflicts between Isrealians and Palestinean.

(c) Americans gained more self-confidence and they were able to judge the new policies more efficiently and participated more cooperatively on issues related with middle east.

5. Macdonald, Lowerence, 2003, "Traditional approaches to citizenship education, globalisation, towards a peace education framework", Ph.D., Dalhousie University, Canada.

Objectives of the study:

1. To compare traditional methods of teaching civics with peace education.
2. To prove that study of peace education is more advantageous than study of civics.

Method: Case study.

Tool: The self made tool was used by the researcher.

Following subjects were included for providing peace education.

(a) Peace education in the form of nuclear war teaching.

(b) Peace education on disarmaments.

(c) Peace education for struggle and conflict resolution.

(d) Peace education and justice.

(e) Globalise education in the form of peace education.

(f) Civics and political science teaching in the form of peace education.

Concept of peace education was advanced to following expected measures:

1. Negative peace.
2. Positive and creative peace.
3. Complete and universal peace with environment.
4. Culture of peace

Result: Peace education is more capable for fulfilling the needs of children of twenty first century than traditional civics teaching because it is more vast, integrated and planned. Although civics teaching is basic element for peace education.

6. Carl Christopher Mirra, 2004, "United States foreign policy since 1945 and the prospects for peace education", Ph.D., Columbia University, U.S.A.

Objective of the study:

The purpose of this work is to examine the prospects for peace education in light of U.S. foreign policy since 1945.

Method: Survey Method.

Result: The conclusion of the study is that American foreign policy presents a significant obstacle to the project of peace education.

7. Sharma Rachnantika, 2006, "Developing a programme on peace education for prospective teachers", M.Ed. dissertation, MLS University, Udaipur.

Objectives of the study:

1. To identify the main components of peace education.
2. To analyse present teachers training programme in context of establishing peace education.
3. To identify need and utility of training of teacher educator.
4. To identify strategies of teaching peace education to teacher educators.
5. To prepare plan of peace education programme for teacher educators.

Method: Survey Method.

Tool: Questionnaire and interview schedule.

Sample: 10 student teachers and one principal from five teachers training colleges.

Result:

(a) For providing peace education teacher should be resourceful and familiar with the concept of peace.

(b) The main elements of peace were identified as love, truth, self control politeness, social justice, economical strength, good health and happiness.

(c) The main elements of peace education were identified as respect for different culture, mutual coordination, faithfulness in democracy, non-violent conflict resolution, protection of human rights.

(d) Measure dimensions of peace education – peace education in context of person, society and environment.

(e) There is no direct content of peace education in theory paper of present teacher training programme.

(f) Student teachers agreed that peace education can be grasped in more efficient manner through co-curricular activities.

(g) New teaching methods are essential for teaching of peace education.

(h) Keeping in view the present syllabus of peace education there is need for modification in present B.Ed. syllabus for would be teachers.

8. E. M. Ajala, 2007, The Impact of Relationship Management of Peace Education on Labour-management Relations and Workers Welfare in Selected Industries in Nigeria, Department of Social Work, University of Ibadan, Ibadan, Nigeria.

Objectives of the study:

1. To what extent would the eleven relationship management of peace education variables, when taken together, predict labour management relations in industries?

2. What are the relative contributions of the variables to the prediction?

Method: Survey Method.

Research Design: The descriptive research design method was adopted for the study.

Sample: Eight industrial unions were purposively selected for the study. From the Distributive sector, 182 participants were selected while 129 participants were selected from the Extractive, 140 participants were selected from Manufacturing Sector while 525 participants were selected from the Service Sector.

Result:

1. Building culture of peace would no doubt have far reaching implications for all field of human interaction in which industrial relations is not the least. This is so because the culture of peace in industries will be based on the principles of freedom, justice and democracy, tolerance and solidarity, respect for all human rights; a culture that rejects violence and, instead, seeks solution to problems through dialogue and negotiation.
2. By helping workers to clarify their values and to explore the implications of the new values. Content of relationship management of peace education should be incorporated into well-defined curriculum which can be used within the work organisations.
3. Workers education curriculum needs to be reviewed to incorporate relationship management of peace education in order to attain a permanent serene environment in industries and reduction in tension and stress.
4. Relationship management of peace education will assist in reducing the intensity of disputes and grievances in the world of work and promotion of workers' welfare.
5. This study finally recommend that the content of relationship management of peace education must be dynamic and functional at industrial levels and should incorporate topics like anger management, strike management, interaction procedure, community building, teams spirit, segmental group

understanding, conflicts, conflict management, conflict resolution, peace, co-operation and interdependence, non-violence, social responsibility, social justice and human rights. All these topics should be included either formally or informally within the work setting.

2.6 Conclusion

Researcher found that a lot of work has been carried out in foreign countries in relation to war affected people and countries. Many studies were conducted on peace-making and peace-keeping forces and their action after war situations. Some articles directly reflect peace as a war preventive idea for human being. Further, some articles discussed the need and benefit of peace education. Some schools are motivating their students and teachers for peace education and enhancing their mind as a peace exploring mind. Some articles discussed the role of peace education for the development of the society. The effect of media activity in maintaining peace among various nations and religions were also discussed in some articles. Few articles proposed human right as a major area of concern.

Most of the studies were carried out in the area of peace and conflict resolution among school children and only one study reflected civics teaching as the basic element for the peace education. A Nigerian study resulted some managerial recommendation that peace education must be dynamic and functional at industrial level and suggests incorporations of various topics formally or informally. In Rajasthan, only one dissertation was found which reflected the need of peace education and suggests that peace education must be a component of B.Ed. syllabus.

Thus, survey of the related literature has proved immensely useful to acquaint the researcher with various articles, researches and studies done in the field of peace education. It shows that not much research work has been carried out in the area of research in teacher education with reference to peace education. Hence, the researcher decided to probe into the study entitled "Developing awareness for the teaching of peace education among prospective teachers."

References

1. Good, C.V. and Douglas E.S. (1954), Methods of Research in Education, Psychology and Sociology, Appleton Century Croft, New York, p. 920.
2. Borg, W.R. and M.D. Gall (1978), Educational Research an Introduction, Mc Graw Hill Book Company, New York, p. 708.
3. Good C.V. (1959), Introduction to Educational Research, Appleton Century Crofts Inc., New York, p. 95.
4. Good C.V. et.al (1945), Educational Research, Appleton Century Crofts Inc., New York, p. 19.
5. Borg R.W. (1963), Educational Research - An Introduction, Longmens Green and Co. Ltd., New York, p. 41.
6. Best John W. (1961), Research in Education, Englewood Clifs, N.J. Prentice Hall, Inc., New York, p. 32.
7. Monisha Bajaj (2010), Conjectures on Peace Education and Gandhian Studies: Method, Institutional Development and Globalisation, Journal of Peace Education, Routledge, London, Volume 7, Issue 1, pp. 47 – 63.
8. Renat Shaykhutdinov (2010), Give Peace a Chance: Non-violent Protest and the Creation of Territorial Autonomy Arrangements, Journal of Peace Research, Sage, London, Vol. 47, No. 2, pp. 179-191.
9. Yaacov Boaz Yablon (2009), Gender Differences in Peace Education Programmes, Gender and Education, Routledge, London, Volume 21, Issue 6, pp. 689 - 701.
10. Pamela Bolotin Joseph, Leslie Smith Duss (2009), Teaching a Pedagogy of Peace: A Study of Peace Educators in United States Schools in the Aftermath of September 11, Journal of

Peace Education, Routledge, London, Volume 6, Issue 2, pp. 189 - 207.

11. Noam Schimmel (2009),Towards a Sustainable and Holistic Model of Peace Education: a Critique of Conventional Modes of Peace Education Through Dialogue in Israel, Journal of Peace Education, Routledge, London, Volume 6, Issue 1, pp. 51 – 68.
12. Candice C. Carter (2008),Voluntary Standards for Peace Education, Journal of Peace Education, Routledge, London, Volume 5, Issue 2, pp. 141 – 155.
13. H.B. Danesh (2008), The Education for Peace Integrative Curriculum: Concepts, Contents and Efficacy, Journal of Peace Education, Routledge, London, Volume 5, Issue 2, pp. 157 – 173.
14. Ole Henning Sommerfelt, Vidar Vambheim (2008), 'The Dream of the Good'- A peace Education Project Exploring the Potential to Educate for Peace at an Individual Level, Journal of Peace Education, Routledge, London, Volume 5, Issue 1, pp. 79–95.
15. Ruth Firer (2008), Virtual Peace Education, Journal of Peace Education, Routledge, London, Volume 5, Issue 2, pp. 193–207.
16. Yaacov Boaz Yablon (2007), Cognitive Rather Than Emotional Modification in Peace Education Programs: Advantages And Limitations, Journal of Moral Education, Routledge, London, Volume 36, Issue 1, pp. 51 – 65.
17. Anita L. Wenden (2007), Educating for a Critically Literate Civil Society: Incorporating the Linguistic Perspective Into Peace Education, Journal of Peace Education, Routledge, London, Volume 4, Issue 2, pp. 163 – 180.
18. David W. Johnson, Roger T. Johnson (2006), Peace Education For Consensual Peace: The Essential Role of Conflict Resolution, Journal of Peace Education, Routledge, London, Volume 3, Issue 2, pp. 147 – 174.
19. H. B. Danesh (2006), To Wards an Integrative Theory of

Peace Education, Journal of Peace Education, Routledge, London, Volume 3, pp. 55 – 78.

20. Johnson, David W., Johnson, Roger T. (2005), Essential Components of Peace Education, Theory Into Practice, Routledge, London, volume 4, pp. 280-292.

21. Kupermintz, Haggai, Salomon Gavriel, (2005), Lessons to Be Learned From Research on Peace Education in the Context of Intractable Conflict, Theory Into Practice, Routledge, London, volume 4 pp. 293-302.

22. Simon Harris, Nick Lewer (2005), Post-graduate peace education in Sri Lanka, Journal of Peace Education, Routledge, London, Volume 2, Issue 2, pp. 109 – 124.

23. Claire McGlynn (2004), Education for peace in integrated schools: a priority for Northern Ireland? Child Care in Practice, Routledge, London, Volume 10, Issue 2, pp. 85-94

24. Gavriel Salomon (2004), Does Peace Education Make a Difference in the Context of an Intractable Conflict? Peace and Conflict: Journal of Peace Psychology, Routledge, London, Volume 10, Issue 3, pp. 257 – 274.

25. Brantmeier, Edward J.(2003), Peace Pedagogy: Exposing and Integrating Peace Education in Teacher Education, Reports-Descriptive; Speeches/Meeting Papers.

26. Bjerstedt, Ake (2003), Developing Preparedness for Peace: Objectives, Methods, Difficulties and Possibilities in Peace-Related Education. Peace Education Reports, Guides - Non-Classroom.

27. Yaacov B. Yablon, Yaacov J. Katz (2001), Internet-Based Group Relations: A High School Peace Education Project in Israel, Educational Media International, Routledge, London, Volume 38, Issue 2 & 3, pp. 175 – 182.

3

Research Design

3.1 Introduction

The present chapter deals with the plan and procedure adopted by the researcher to achieve the aims and objectives of the study.

3.2 Research Design of the Study

Research design occupies a key position in the research work. It is based on the research purpose, like exploration, description, diagnosis and experimentation. Research design means the exact nature of the research work in a systematic manner. It involves the information about the research work in view of framework of study, availability of various data, observations, analysis, sampling, etc. Research design includes the structure of research work and helps the researcher to organise his/her ideas in a particular form.

"Research design is a mapping strategy. It is essentialay a statement of the objectives of the inquiry and the strategies for collecting the evidences, analysing the evidences and reporting the findings".[1]

"Research design is a plan, structure and strategy of investigation so conceived as to obtain answers to research questions and to control variance".[2]

Thus, research design is primarily data discipline. The main purpose of all research designs is to impose control over relevant variables and thus allow the operation of the experimental variable at the level of maximum saturation. This is the ideal, which all scientific investigations try to approximate as closely as possible. It is tried by adopting and approximating a sound strategy of control over relevant variables that affect the dependable variable (D.V.). Otherwise they are likely to contaminate the effect of the independent variable (I.V.). When these sources of relevant or extraneous or error variances, pertaining to the particular research problem under study, have been properly controlled the design is said to possess internal validity. Concomitant planning on an appropriate structure is also undertaken. The structure of a research design investigation is more specific than the strategy or plan part of a research design. It implies selection of a paradigm or model or the scheme of operation of the variables.

Every research design should also be externally valid. External validity implies manipulation of the experimental variables and control of the extraneous and error variables to such a magnitude that the independent variable (I.V.) is able to be effective in a fully saturated manner to lead to generalised results.

The main technical function of research design is to control variance. A research design is a manner of speaking, a set of instructions to the investigator to gather and analyse his data in certain ways. It is, therefore, a control mechanism. The statistical principle behind the mechanism is, maximise (max) systematic variance, minimise (min) error variance and control (con) extraneous variances.[3]

Following Table shows the details of research design:

Independent variable	*Dependent variable*	
Groups	*Pre experimental stage*	*Post experimental stage*
1.Experimental Group (Teaching package) (N= 100)	Measurement of awareness of teaching of peace education	Measurement of awareness of teaching of peace education
2.Control Group (Normal Activity) (N= 100)	Measurement of awareness of teaching of peace education	Measurement of awareness of teaching of peace education

3.3 Methodology of the Study

Experimental method is a scientific method. It is oriented to the future in the sense that the researcher is seeking to evaluate something new. There are many views about the experimental method given by different authors. Some are given below:

Experimental method provides for much control and, therefore, establishes a systematic and logical association between manipulated factors and observed effects. The researcher defines a problem and proposes a tentative answer or hypothesis. He tests the hypothesis and accepts or rejects it in the light of the controlled variable relationship that he has observed.[4]

"When certain variables can be controlled or manipulated directly in a research problem by the investigator, the research procedure is often described as an experiment."[5]

In the opinion of Best, J.W. "Experimental research is the description and analysis of what will occur under carefully controlled conditions".[6]

The role of methodology is to carry out the research work in a scientific manner. To conduct the present research, the researcher has used experimental method.

3.4 Variables

Variables are concepts that have been operationalised. Operationalisation is the specification of unambiguous measurement procedure that, when applied, results in a numerical value for the concept for each case or observation in the study. Those values are data that are nominal, ordinal, interval or ratio level.

There are two big categories of variables i.e., independent and dependent variables. Unlike levels of data, a concept is not inherently one type of variable or the other. Rather a variable is independent or dependent, depends on the research question and hypotheses. In one study, a concept may be an independent variable, while in another study the same may be a dependent variable.

(a) *Dependent Variable*- A dependent variable is a concept that is impacted or influenced by other variables in the study. Those other values are independent variables. The value of dependent variable depends upon the value of the relevant independent variables. The dependent variable is typically the concept, which the researcher is trying to describe, explain and predict.

(b) *Independent Variable*- Independent variable is directly manipulated by the researcher; the changes that occur in the dependent variable are observed and measured. There are two kinds of independent variables;

  (a) manipulated independent variables and

  (b) non-manipulated independent variables.

  Manipulated independent variables are those that the experimenter controls by active manipulation. Non-manipulated independent variables are variables that are not directly under the experimenter's control.

(c) *Extraneous Variable*: The independent variable which affects the dependent variable and, does not pertain to the subject matter, is called extraneous variable.

In this investigation the teaching package of peace education was taken as independent variable. Two groups were used, each for separate experimental treatment. Experimental group consisted of subjects who were given the teaching package for three weeks and control group consisted of subjects who underwent normal activity for the same span of time. Awareness for the teaching of peace education was taken as dependent variable.

3.5 Hypothesis

When a researcher observes known facts and takes up a problem for analysis he has to start somewhere and this start is the hypothesis. A hypothesis is a proposition that is stated in testable forms and predicts a particular relationship between two (or more) variables. It is provisional formulation or possible solution or tentative explanation or suggested answer to the problem being faced by the researcher. Hypothesis presents more specific and clearly testable statements which are indicative of the expected results.

Hypothesis is a suggested answer to the problem under investigation.

Null Hypothesis (Ho)

Null hypothesis states a zero difference or no difference between the values of two variables, or a zero relationship between them.

In this study researcher used null hypotheses for finding the effectiveness of teaching package of peace education. The null hypotheses are as follows -

1. There is no significant difference between the control and experimental groups of prospective teachers with regard to the awareness of teaching of peace education before administrating the teaching package.
2. There is no significant difference between the control and experimental groups of prospective teachers with regard to the awareness of teaching of peace education after administrating the teaching package.
3. There is no significant difference between the experimental group of prospective teachers with regard to the awareness of teaching of peace education before and after the administration of the teaching package.
4. There is no significant difference between the control group of prospective teachers with regard to the awareness of teaching of peace education before and after the administration of the teaching package.

3.6 Sample

To see the efficacy of teaching package for developing awareness of teaching of peace education among prospective teachers in this investigation a purposive sample of two hundred prospective teachers was used as total subjects. Sample was selected from two teachers training colleges of Udaipur

(Rajasthan). Among the sample two groups were formed:

(a) *Experimental group:* This group underwent teaching package of peace education for three weeks regularly.

(b) *Control group*: This group underwent normal activity for equal span of time.

Cross check sampling was taken to nullify difference, if any, between the two institutes from which the subjects of experimental groups and control groups were selected.

In each college, half of the students were randomly selected for experimental group and other half were selected as a control group i.e., from college A, a group of 50 prospective teachers was selected for control group (Con A) and another group of 50 prospective teachers was selected for experimental group (Exp A). Similarly, from college B, a group of 50 prospective teachers was selected for control group (Con B) and another group of 50 prospective teachers was selected for experimental group (Exp B).

The following diagram clarifies the sample of the study:

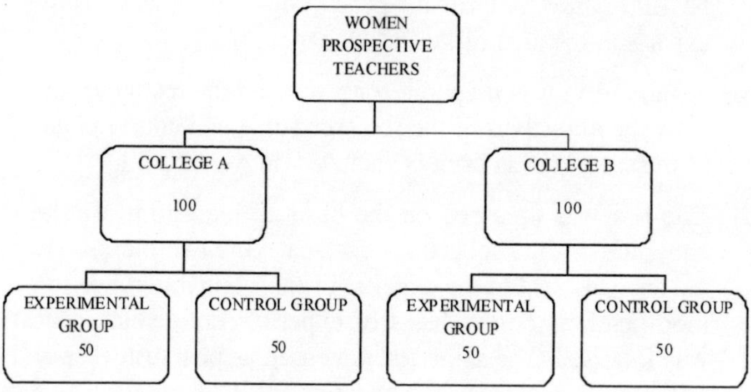

Characteristics of the subject

1. Experimental and control group - The subjects of both the

groups were women candidates pursuing B.Ed. course. They were admitted through pre-teachers' entrance test conducted by J.N.V. University, Jodhpur, Rajasthan.

2. Both the teachers colleges are recognised by National Council of Teacher Education and affiliated to Mohan Lal Sukhadiya University, Udaipur.

3.7 Tool

The following tools were used by the researcher:

A. Self Made Test

Self made test was developed and used for measuring the awareness of teaching of peace education among prospective teachers.

Steps for Preparing Test

The following steps were applied for preparing test:

(a) The researcher designed a course content consisting of some units on peace education. For developing the course content, the researcher referred to some training material prepared by NCERT and UNICEF on peace education and consulted experts in the area of Peace Education.

(b) A blue print was prepared for preparing the test keeping in view the objectives of the research study and course content of the study. (Blue print is enclosed in Annexure 1)

(c) The test was prepared on the basis of blue print. The test consisted of thirty questions each carrying two marks. Then the test was sent to the experts for their opinion. After some modifications on the basis of experts' comments, pre-test was finalised. The same test was used as post test. (Pre-and post-test is enclosed in Annexure 2)

(d) An answer sheet was prepared for calculating the test score of the test taken for measuring the awareness of teaching of peace education among prospective teachers.

(e) Preliminary try out - The prepared test was administered on a small sample of ten women prospective teachers of Jyotiba Phule Teachers Training College, Udaipur and it was found that test items were easily understood by them. So, the test was applicable on the complete sample as per research design.

B. Teaching Package

The researcher used the following steps for preparing the teaching package:

(a) Selection of the teaching unit

After consultation with subject experts, some units on peace education were selected and some literature on peace education was also taken into consideration. Finally after consulting with the guide, final six units were selected.

(b) Selection of the outline of the teaching unit

To draft the outline of the teaching package some content material for the teaching package was prepared. For this purpose training course on peace education for teachers' by NCERT and some books related to topics of teaching package were referred.

(c) Inviting opinion of the expert on teaching package

After preparing the teaching package it was sent to the experts for their opinion. After considering and including the advice and comments of the experts, the teaching package was finalised. (a sample of one unit of teaching package is enclosed in Annexure 3)

(d) Areas of Teaching Package

The measure areas considered in teaching package are as follows:

(a) Peace education – need importance and meaning

(b) Human rights – fundamental rights of the child

(c) Fundamental duties –according to constitution

(d) Child rights

(e) Disarmaments

(f) The behavioural pattern and its implementation for peace education

C. Interview Schedule

A semi-structured interview schedule was designed by the researcher to find out the opinion of the principals (teachers college) and experts on developing awareness for teaching of peace education among the prospective teachers.

(Semi-structured interview schedule is enclosed in Annexure 4)

3.8 Procedure

Following procedure was adopted by the research to carry out his investigation:

(I) Pre-testing

The self made pre-test was administered on the subjects of all the groups, prior to assigning their respective treatments.

(II) Teaching of peace education through teaching package to Experimental Group

After conducting and evaluating the result of pre-test, the subjects of experimental group were taught peace education by the teaching package. The teaching was imparted by the researcher himself. The teaching was done for the duration of an hour in a day for three weeks regularly.

(III) Control Group

No specific treatment was given to Control Group. They were indulged in their normal daily activities for the three weeks period of experimental treatment.

(IV) Post-testing

After three weeks of their respective treatments, all the subjects of both the groups were again tested i.e., post-test was administered on the subjects of experimental as well as control group.

3.9 Statistical Design

Any adequately designed experimental study assumes a back up of appropriate statistical design. The experimental design represents a method of scientific data collection while the statistical design represents a method of data analysis whereby inference drawing and hypothesis testing become possible. The whole exercise of developing an adequate research design is like creating a balance between the two sides of the same coin of research design.

To compare the effect of independent variables (IV) on the subjects of both groups the following statistical design was adopted:

(i) Inter- group Comparison

To evaluate the significant effect of the intervention on the subjects of experimental group and normal activity on subjects of control group the students 't' test was employed with a criterion on α = or $p< 0.05$.

YEb X YCb

R-

YEa X YCa

The 't' value has been calculated on the basis of the book Principal and Methods of Psychology written by Lawson R.B., Goldstein S.G. and Musty R.E.[7].

(ii) Intra-group Comparison

To evaluate the effect of respective interventions in the subjects of control and experimental groups (within the groups) Sandlers 'A' test with criterion of α = or $p< 0.05$ was used, as the Sandlers 'A' test is quite economic with regard to time and accurate test for comparing the subjects within the groups.

YEb X YEa

R-

YCb X YCa

The 'A' value has been calculated on the basis of the book Elements of Statistics written by Kapil H.K.[8]

3.10 Conclusion

This chapter deals with research design and methodology of the study. It also discusses variables and states the hypotheses used in the study. Sample and tools used in the study are also described in the chapter. It also discusses the procedure of the study in detail. At the end statistical design is given for comparing the effect of independent variable on the subject of experimental as well as control groups.

References

1. Sharma, R.A. (2009), Education Research, R. Lal Book Depo, Meerut, p. 151.
2. Kerlinger, F.N. (1983), Foundation of Behavioural Research, Education and Psychological Inquiry, Holt Rinehart and Winston, New York.
3. *Ibid*, p. 306.
4. Chandra, S.S. and Sharma R.K.(2007), Research in Education, Atlantic Publishers and Distributors, New Delhi, p. 353.
5. Shrivastava, D.N.(1981), Anusandhan vidhiya,Sahitya Prakashan, Agra, p. 127.
6. Best, J.W. (1963), Research in Education, Prentice Hall of India, New Delhi, p. 125.
7. Lawson, R.B., Goldstein S.G.I. and Musty R.E. (1975), Principal and Methods of Psychology, Oxford University Press, London.
8. Kapil H.K.(1981), Elements of Statistics, Vinod Pustak Mandir, Agra.

4

Analysis and Interpretation of the Data

4.1 Introduction

It is very essential in research to analyse and interpret the collected data scientifically. Scientifically means a systematic observation of collected data in tabular form.

According to Good, Barr and Scates: The process of interpretation is essentially one of the stating what the findings shows? What do they mean? What is their significance? What is the original problem? That all the limitations of data must enter into and become a part of interpretation of the results.

Appropriate interpretations are very necessary to make a selection, administration and scoring worth-while. Interpretation needs critical examination of the results of the analysed data, which means the study of the tabulated material in order to determine facts or meaning. It involves breaking down existing complex factors into simpler parts and putting that part together in new arrangements for the purpose of the interpretation.

In the present chapter the aim of the investigation is to analyse and interpret the data after collecting it through experimentation as described in the previous chapter. The analysis and interpretation of the data enable the researcher to arrive at certain definite conclusions.

4.2 Interpretation of Data

In continuation of the previous outline drawn by the researcher, the following output is obtained-

1. The mean scores of all the experimental and control groups at pre-experimental stage are given below:

Group	*Pre-Test score*
Control A	8.48
Control B	11.76
Experimental A	12.43
Experimental B	8.92

Looking at the pre-test scores it was realised that the performance of all groups were not up to the mark and their awareness towards teaching of peace education was far below. The graphical representation of the above data is presented below:

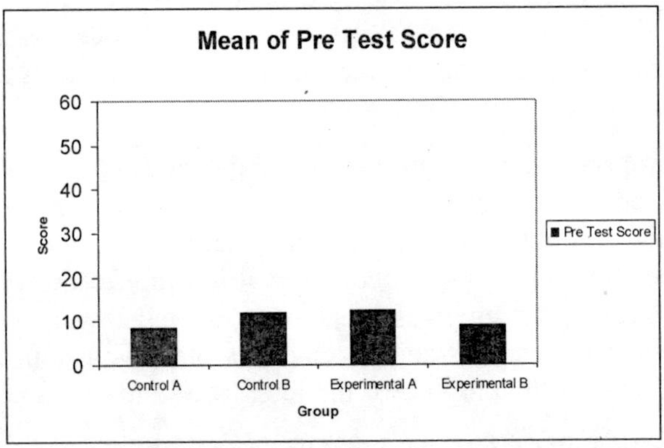

Figure -1. The mean scores of all the groups at pre-experimental stage.

Here, it is clear that there is an urgent need for developing awareness for teaching of peace education among prospective teachers.

2. To develop awareness for teaching of peace education among prospective teachers the subjects of experimental group were taught peace education by the teaching package. The control group was indulged in their normal daily activities for a period of three weeks during experimental treatment.

At the end of the experiment, post-test was administered on the subjects of all the groups. The post-test scores are given below:

Groups	*Post-test score*
Control A	9.3
Control B	12.18
Experimental A	31.78
Experimental B	37.92

The table clearly shows the difference of scores of experimental group and control group. The graphical representation of the data in table is presented below:

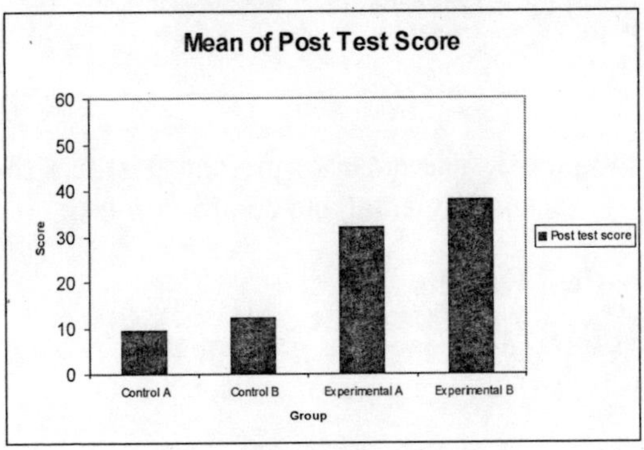

Figure -2. The mean scores of all the groups at post-experimental stage.

3. The comparison of mean of pre and post test scores of experimental and control groups are as follows :

Groups	*Pre-test score*	*Post-test score*
Control A+ Control B	10.12	10.675
Experimental A+ Experimental B	10.74	34.85

The above scores are shown in the graph given below, indicates again of scores in the experimental group in comparison to the control group.

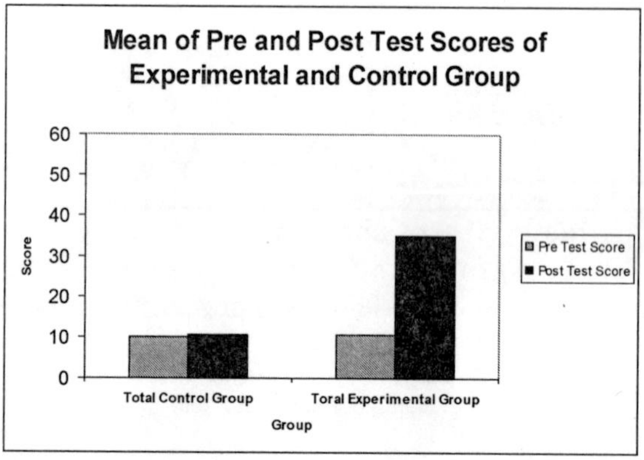

Figure-3. The mean of pre-and post-test scores of experimental and control groups.

4.3 Statistical Results

Here, intra-group and inter-group analysis strategy is adopted for analysis and interpretation of collected data.

A. Inter-group comparison

(a) Pre-experimental stage

At pre-experimental stage, the level of experimental and

control group was analysed to see the homogeneity among the groups. Here, a two tailed student t test with with $p \leq 0.05$ and $p \leq 0.01$ was applied to test the significance of difference among the groups.

Table-1

Mean, S.D. and 't' values for experimental and control groups at Pre-Experimental stage (N=100 for each group)

Groups	*Mean*	*S.D.*	*T*	*p<*
Experimental	10.675	7.5234	0.4811	N.S.
Control	10.12	9.37979		

The study of Table 1 reveals that the means of pre-test scores of experimental and control group are 10.675 and 10.12 respectively. The calculated value of t is 0.4811 which is not significant at 0.05 and 0.01 level of confidence. Thus, the value of t indicates that the two groups viz., experimental and control groups are similar so far as the awareness of teaching of peace education is concerned, i.e. the subject of both groups are homogeneous when it comes to the awareness of teaching of peace education, as there is no significant difference between the mean scores of both the groups. Here, the obtained result is in tune with the null hypothesis no.1 proposed earlier.

The graphical representation of the data and the difference between the mean score in this case are as follows:

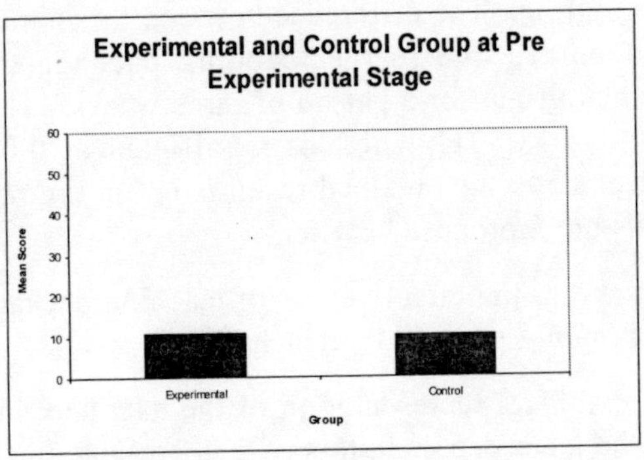

Figure - 4. Experimental and control group at pre-experimental stage.

(b) Post-experimental stage

At post-experimental stage, the level of the experimental and control group was analysed to see the significant difference if any, occurring in the awareness of teaching of peace education in the subjects of experimental group after giving intervention of peace education package for three weeks as compared to the subject of control groups indulged in their normal activity for the same span of time. Here, a two tailed t test with with $p \leq 0.05$ and $p \leq 0.01$ was applied to was applied to test the significance of difference among the groups.

Table-2

Mean, S.D. and 't' values for experimental and control groups at Post-Experimental stage (N=100 for each group)

Groups	*Mean*	*S.D.*	*t*	*p<*
Experimental	34.85	8.74428	18.8211	0.005
Control	10.74	8.72425		

The study of Table 2 reveals that the means of pre-test scores of experimental and control group are 34.85 and 10.74 respectively. The difference between means is 24.11. This difference between the two means shows the superiority of experimental group over the control group. The difference between the marks of the two groups occurred due to the teaching package given to the experimental group for a period of three weeks. The calculated value of t is 18.8211 which is significant at 0.005 level of confidence. Here, the obtained result is not in tune with the null hypothesis no. 2 proposed earlier.

This shows the effectiveness of teaching package for peace education among prospective teachers.

The graphical representation of the data and the difference between the mean scores in this case is presented below:

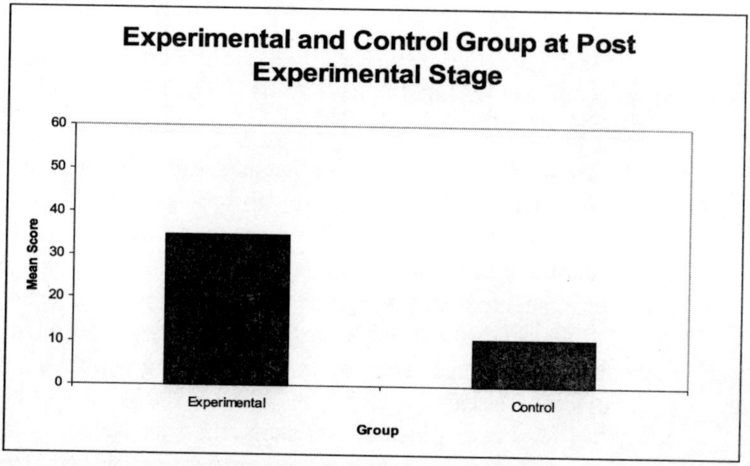

Figure - 5. Experimental and control group at post-experimental stage.

B. Intra-group comparison

Intra-group comparison is made between pre-and post-tests of the experimental group and pre-and post-test of control group. To evaluate the effect of respective interventions in the subjects of control and experimental groups (within the groups) Sandlers 'A' test with criterion of $\alpha =$ or $p< 0.05$ was used. The Sandlers 'A' test is economic with regard to time and accurate test for comparing the subjects within the groups.

(a) Experimental Group

In this section collected data of pre-test for the awareness of teaching of peace education in the subjects of experimental group were compared with the data of post-test (within the group) after giving intervention of peace education package for three weeks. Sandlers 'A' test with criterion of $\alpha =$ or $p < 0.05$ was used.

Table-3

Mean and Sandler's 'A' value of the subjects of the experimental group (N=100 for each group)

Mean		*'A'*	*P <*
Pre test	Post test		
10.675	34.85	0.012007	P < .001

The study of Table 3 reveals that the means of pre-test scores and post-test scores of experimental groups are 10.675 and 34.85 respectively. The difference between means is 24.175. This difference between the two means shows the superiority of post-test scores of experimental group over the pre-test scores of the experimental group. The difference between the scores of the two stages occurred due to the teaching package given to the experimental group for a period of three weeks. The calculated value of 'A' is 0.012007 which is significant at 0.001 level of confidence. This shows the effectiveness of teaching package for peace education among prospective teachers. Here, the obtained result rejects the null hypothesis no. 3 proposed earlier.

The graphical representation of the data and the difference between the mean scores in this case is presented below:

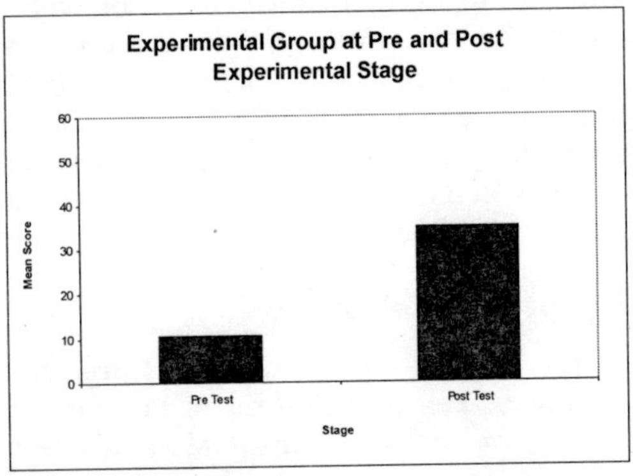

Figure - 6. Experimental group at pre-and post-experimental stage.

(b) Control Group

The mean scores of control group obtained at pre-experimental stage are compared with post-experimental stage to find out significant difference, if any, between the two stages. It has already been mentioned earlier that the subjects of control group were not initiated to any assignment and they were doing their normal activities. To evaluate the difference between the two stages, Sandlers 'A' test with criterion of α = or p< 0.05 was used.

Table-4

Mean and Sandlers 'A' value of the subjects of the Control Group (N=100 for each group)

Mean		*'A'*	*P*
Pre-test	Post-test		
10.12	10.74	0.947841	N.S.

The study of Table 4 reveals that the means of pre-test scores and post-test scores of control group are 10.12 and 10.74 respectively. The calculated value of 'A' is 0.947841 which is not significant at 0.05 level of confidence. Here, the obtained result is in tune with the null hypothesis no. 4 proposed earlier.

The graphical representation of the data and the difference between the mean scores in this case is presented below:

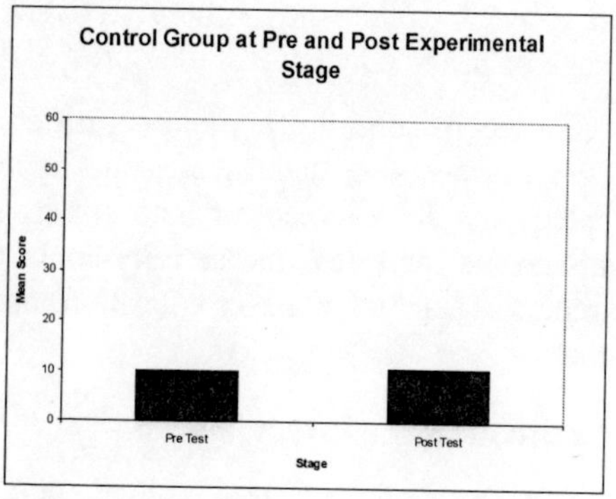

Figure - 7. Control group at pre-and post-experimental stage.

The Table - 4 and Figure - 7 reveals that there is no significant difference between the scores of two experimental stages i.e., pre-and post. This indicates that the subjects of control group could not develop any attitude towards peace development.

4.4 Discussion

These results lead to following conclusions with respect to the original hypotheses:

(i) The subjects of experimental group did not differ significantly at pre-experimental stage from those of control group. This means the awareness of teaching of peace education in all the subjects was homogeneous at this stage. Here, the first hypothesis is confirmed by this finding.

(ii) The subjects of experimental group differ significantly at post-experimental stage from those of control group. Here, null hypothesis no. 2 is rejected. The difference between the marks of the two groups occurred due to the teaching package given to the experimental group for a period of three weeks. This shows the effectiveness of teaching package for peace education among prospective teachers.

(iii) The subjects of experimental group differ significantly at pre-test and post-test stage. Here, null hypothesis no. 3 is rejected. The difference between the marks of the two groups occurred due to the teaching package given to the subjects for a period of three weeks. This shows the effectiveness of teaching package of peace education among prospective teachers.

(iv) The subjects of control group did not differ significantly at pre-test and post-test stage. Here, null hypothesis no. 4 is accepted. The achievement of both groups is similar. This means normal daily routine activity could not change the awareness of teaching of peace education among prospective teachers.

4.5 Findings through the Interview

Interview technique was also used by the researcher for getting information from the experts in the area of peace education to know their opinion on the main objectives of the present research work. Major findings of the interview are as below –

1. Spreading awareness for developing peace education among prospective teachers is the need of the hour.
2. Every educational institute must promote peace education programmes as an integral component in their curriculum.
3. Prospective teachers should understand the meaning of peace. They should lead peaceful life and should promote and inculcate peace values in their students.
4. Prospective teachers should spread the value of equality and social justice on the basis of moral and social ethics.
5. Prospective teachers should encourage peace values and discourage casteism. They should also run a reading club in their institutions which will promote peace activities.
6. Child centred methodology is the most effective way for promoting peace education among our students.
7. Experts are of the opinion that workshops and seminars should be organised on peace education for prospective teachers in teachers training institutes.
8. Prospective teachers should guide their students to view and listen creative and peace based programmes from mass media and should also discourage the spreading of violence being spread by mass media.
9. The child should not suffer because of conflicts between parents and teachers.
10. Teachers should select peace values from the content areas and should impart those values to their students through their teaching learning process.
11. Experts feel that the prospective teachers should undergo an orientation programme for peace education, so that they are able to inculcate peace value among their students.

Findings of interview also support the results of researcher's investigation. So, it can be concluded that there is an urgent need to develop awareness for the teaching of peace education among prospective teachers and, for this the teaching package used in this research can work as a guide to our teacher education institutions.

4.6 Conclusion

This chapter deals with analysis and interpretation of data. Researcher tries to analyse the data in a systematic manner and discusses the results. The inter-group comparison and intra-group comparison is discussed as per the design of the research. The data table and graphical representation is also given at appropriate place. At the end, the researcher presents the findings through the interview of various experts in the field of education.

5

Conclusion, Educational Implication and Suggestions

5.1 Introduction

This chapter deals with the conclusion and educational implication of the present research work. It also includes suggestions for the further researches.

5.2 Conclusion of the Study

The present experimental study aims at evaluating the effectiveness of developing awareness for teaching of peace education among prospective teachers.

(a) Conclusion drawn from the experiment

The researcher prepared a teaching package for developing awareness for teaching of peace education among prospective teachers and conducted an experiment (teaching work) to evaluate whether this experiment has made any significant difference in the prospective teachers.

According to the requirement of the study, the researcher divided the sample into two groups (experimental and control). The researcher administered the teaching package on the experimental group for a period of three weeks and no treatment was given to the control group, rather they were indulged in their normal activity for equal interval of time.

The investigator has not made any hasty generalisation and he was well-aware of the limited sample and the content of the teaching package which he taught to the experimental group for a limited period of three weeks.

Following are the conclusions drawn from the data obtained in the present experiment:

1. The mean scores at pre-test stage of the experimental and the control groups were homogeneous and very low. Therefore, the awareness towards teaching of peace education of the subjects of both experimental and control group was very low at initial level. So, it can be concluded that there is a need for development of awareness for the teaching of peace education among prospective teachers.
2. The mean scores at post-test stage of control group did not differ significantly in comparison to pre-test stage. It suggests that normal daily routine activities could not change the awareness for teaching of peace education among prospective teachers.
3. After administrating the teaching package to the experimental group, significant difference was found in the mean scores at pre-and post-test stage. The difference between the scores of the two stages occurred due to the teaching based on teaching package given to the experimental group for a period of three weeks. This shows the effectiveness of teaching based on teaching package for peace education among prospective teachers.

(b) Conclusions drawn from the interview schedule

Interview technique was also used by the researcher for getting information from the experts in the area of peace education to know their opinion on the main objectives of the present research work. Major findings of the interview are as below :

1. Spreading awareness for developing peace education among prospective teachers is the need of the hour.
2. Every educational institute must promote peace education programmes as an integral component in their curriculum.
3. Prospective teachers should understand the meaning of peace. They should lead peaceful life and should promote and inculcate peace values in their students.
4. Prospective teachers should spread the value of equality and social justice on the basis of moral and social ethics.
5. Prospective teachers should encourage peace values and discourage casteism. They should also run a reading club in their institutions which will promote peace activities.
6. Child centred methodology is the most effective way for promoting peace education among our students.
7. Experts are of the opinion that workshops and seminars should be organised on peace education for prospective teachers in teachers training institutes.
8. Prospective teachers should guide their students to view and listen creative and peace based programmes from mass media and should also discourage the spreading of violence being spread by mass media.
9. The child should not suffer because of conflicts between parents and teachers.
10. Teachers should select peace values from the content areas and should impart those values to their students through their teaching learning process.
11. Experts feel that the prospective teachers should undergo an orientation programme for peace education, so that they are able to inculcate peace value among their students.

Findings of interview also support the results of researcher's investigation. So, it can be concluded that there is an urgent need to develop awareness for the teaching of peace education among prospective teachers and, for this the teaching package used in this research can work as a guide to our teacher education institutions.

5.3 Educational Implication

National curriculum framework 2005 emphasised the importance of peace education. UNESCO is also considering peace education as an important area. Currently National Curriculum Framework for Teacher Education 2009 has emphasised the importance of peace education in teachers' training programme. Above facts reflect that this research will act as a pioneer in the field of education. Educational implication of the present research work is given below:

(a) For Teacher Education Institutes

Teacher education institutes can work for development of peace culture through various research works as suggested by the researcher.

(b) For Teacher Educators

The research suggests that teacher educators should also be oriented for peace education by means of training programme in the field of teaching of peace education.

(c) For School Teachers

This teaching package developed by the researcher will also act as a guide to the in-service programme for developing awareness for the teaching of peace education among regular teachers working in the schools.

(d) For Students

Students are the prospective citizens and if the teachers are oriented for developing peace culture then automatically it will prevail among the students.

5.4 Suggestions for Further Research

The researcher tried to give his best in the area of peace education. Further, there are some major areas left which can be selected by the future researchers for further studies. Some of them are suggested below:

1. Study of attitudes of teacher educators towards peace education.
2. Comparative study of peace teaching attitude of pre-service and in-service teachers.
3. Development of a code of professional ethics of peace education among teachers.
4. Study of training needs for peace education for the heads of teacher education institutions and developing a training programme for peace education.
5. Development of a peace education curriculum framework for prospective teachers.
6. Action researches on different problems related with teaching of peace education.
7. Study of problems faced by teachers acting as peace educators.
8. Developing a teaching model for pre-school teachers to create a culture of peace in pre-school institutions.
9. Role of parent/teacher co-operation for developing peace culture among students.
10. Development of awareness for peace education among faculty members of academic colleges.

5.5 Conclusion

This chapter deals with the conclusion of the present study which is given in two parts namely, conclusion drawn from the experiment and conclusion drawn from the interview schedule. The educational implication of the present research work and suggestions for further researches are also given in this chapter.

Bibliography

Books and Reports

Aggrawal, A. (2000), Indian Ocean and World Peace, Kanishka Publisher, New Delhi.

Aggrawal, Y.P. (1998), The Science of Educational Research, Nirmal Book Agency, Kurukshetra.

Aggrawal, J.C. (1973), Educational Research and Introduction, Arya Book Depot, New Delhi.

Aggrawal, J.C. (2005), Education for Values, Environment and Human Rights, Shipra Publications, Delhi.

Altman Nathaniel, (1988), The Nonviolent Revolution, Element Books Ltd., Worcester, Great Britain.

Ary Donald et. al (1972), Introduction to Research in Education, Halt Rinchart and Winston Inc., New York.

Avinashilingam, T.S. (1971), Education, Ramkrishna Mission, Coimbatore.

Bagchi, J.P. and Teckchandani, V. (2005), Values Education, University Book House (P) Ltd., Jaipur.

Balasooriya, A.S. (2001), Learning the Way of Peace: A Teachers' Guide to Peace Education, UNESCO, New Delhi.

Balsara, M. (1996), New Education Policy and Developmental Challenges, Kanishka Publishers, New Delhi.

Best, J.W. (1961), Research in Education, Englewood Cliffs, N.J. Prentice Hall, Inc., New York.

Best, J.W. (1963), Research in Education, Prentice Hall of India Pvt. Ltd, New Delhi.

Best, J.W. (2007), Research in Education, Prentice Hall of India Pvt. Ltd, New Delhi.

Best, J.W. and Kahn, J.V. (1992), Research in Education, Prentice Hall of India Pvt. Ltd., New Delhi.

Best, J.W. and Kahn, J.V. (2007), Research in Education, Prentice Hall of India, New Delhi.

Bey, T.M. and Gwendolyn, Y.T. (1996), Making School a Place of Peace, Corwin Press, Inc. Thousand Oaks, California.

Bhattacharya, S. (2002), Foundations of Education, Atlantic Publisher and Distributors, New Delhi.

Borg, W.R. (1963), Educational Research - An Introduction, Longmans Green and Co. Ltd., New York.

Borg, W.R. and Gall, M.D. (1963), Educational Research - an Introduction, Longman Green and Co. Ltd., New York.

Borg, W.R. and Gall, M.D. (1978), Educational Research - an Introduction, Mc Graw Hill Book Company, New York.

Bose, A. (1981), Dimensions of Peace and Non Violence, Gian Publishing House, New Delhi.

Carter, V.G. (1945), Dictionary of Education, McGraw-Hill, New York.

Catherine, H. (1997), Research Design, Routledge, London.

Chandra, S.S. and Sharma, R.K.(2007), Research in Education, Atlantic Publisher and Distributor, New Delhi.

Chattopadhyay, S.N. (2001), Swami Vivekananda: His Global Vision. Punthi Pustak, Kolkata.

Cohen, L. et. al (2006), Research Methods in Education, Routledge, London.

Dalai, Lama (1980), Universal Responsibility and the Good Heart, Library of Tibetan Works and Archives, Dharamshala, H.P.

Dalai, Lama (1997), Love, Kindness and Universal Responsibility, Paljor Publications, New Delhi.

Dalai, Lama (1999), Book of Wisdom, Thorsons Publications, London.

Dalal, A.S. (2000), Growing Within: The Psychology of Inner Development, Sri Aurobindo Ashram, New Delhi.

Dasgupta, S. (1961), Tagore's Asian Outlook, Nava Bharati, Kolkata.

Delors, J. (1996), Learning the Treasure Within, UNESCO Publishing, Paris, France.

Dhankar, R. (2007), Shiksha, Viveksheelta Aur Mataropan (in Hindi) Maharishi Valmiki College of Education, Delhi University, New Delhi.

Dhokalia, R.P. (2001), Eternal Human Values and World Religions. New Delhi: National Council of Educational Research and Training, New Delhi.

Dhondial, S.N. and Phatak, A.B. (1972), Shiksha Anusandhan Ka Vidhishastra, Rajasthan Hindi Granth Academy, Jaipur.

Diwakar, R.R. (1989), Nehru and His Contribution to World Peace, Gandhi Peace Foundation, New Delhi.

Duggar, B.R. (2008), Vishva Shanti avm Ahinsa Prashikshan, Acharya Shanti Sagar Chani Smriti Granthmala, Muzaage affarnagar,U.P.

Fountain, S. (1999), Peace Education in UNICEF, New York: Working Paper, Education Section, Programme Division, UNICEF.

Gage, N.L. (1965), A Handbook of Research on Teaching, The American Educational Research Association, Ronald M.C. Nally and Company, Chicago.

Galtung, J. (1984), The Struggle for Peace, Peace Research Centre, Gujrat Vidyapeeth, Ahmedabad.

Gandhi, M.K. (1999), Character and Nation Building, Navjeevan Publishing House, Ahmedabad.

Gangrade, K.D. (2001), Religion and Peace, A Gandhian Perspective, Gandhi Smriti and Darshan Samiti, New Delhi.

Garrett, E.H. (2007), Statistics in Psychology and Education, Kalyani Publisher, Ludhiyana.

Ghosh, P.S. et.al (2000), Pluralism and Equality - Values in Indian Society and Politics. Sage Publications, New Delhi.

Good, C.V. (1959), Introduction to Educational Research, Appleton Century Crofts, New York.

Good, C.V. and Douglas E.S. (1954), Methods of Research in Education, Psychology and Sociology, Appleton Century Crofts, New York.

Good, C.V. et. al (1945), Educational Research, Appleton Century Crofts Inc., New York.

Government of India (1960), Report of the committee on religious and moral instruction, New Delhi.

Guillford, J.P. (1942), Fundamental Statistics in Psychology and Education, Mc Graw Hill Book Company, New York.

Gupta, S.C. and Kapoor, V.K. (1970), Fundamentals of Mathematical Statistics, S. Chand and Company, New Delhi.

Gyatso, T. (1995), Opening the Mind and Generating a Good Health, The Fourteenth Dalai Lama Publisher Library of Tibetan Works and Archives.

Gyatso, T. (1995), Universal Responsibility and the Good Health, Library of Tibetan Works and Archives, Dharamshala, H.P.

Hant, T. N. (2004), Being Peace By Nice Printing Press, Delhi.

Harris, I.M. (1998), Peace Education, McFarland, North Carolina.

Harris, I.M. and Morrison, M.L. (2003), Peace Education,

Second Edition, McFarland and Company, Inc., Publishers, Jefferson, North Carolina.

Hildreth, H. and Ashan, M.C. (1963), Elements of Educational Research, Mc Graw Hill Book Company, New York.

Hill-way, T.H. (1966), Introduction to Research, Houghton Miffin Company, Bosten.

Hudson, Dale L. (1992), New Tools for International Understanding: a Peace Education Curriculum for Elementary School Students. Hawaii: Spark M. Matsunaga Institute for Peace, University of Hawaii, Manoa.

Jagadeesan (1998), Everyday Human Values, Sterling Publishers (P) Ltd., New Delhi.

Jain, G.L. (2003), Research Methodology, Mangaldeep Publications, Jaipur.

Juergensmeyer, M. (2003), Gandhi's way - A Handbook of Conflict Resolution, Oxford University Press, London.

Kagan, Spencer (1994), Cooperative Learning, San Juan Capistrano; Kagan Enterprises, California.

Kapil, K.H.(1981), Elements of Statistics, Vinod Pustak Mandir, Agra.

Kaur, B. (2006), Teaching of Peace and Conflict and Pride - School Histories of the Freedom Struggle in India, Penguin Books India Pvt. Ltd., New Delhi.

Kerlinger, F.N. (1986), Foundation of Behavioural Research, Education and Psychological Inquiry, Holt Rinehart and Winston, New York.

Kothari, L.S. (2001), Education for Peace. Gandhi Smriti and Darshan Samiti, New Delhi.

Koul, L. (1999), Methodology of Educational Research, Vikas Publishing House Pvt. Ltd. New Delhi.

Krishnamurti, J. (1973), Beyond Violence, Krishnamurti Foundation, Chennai.

Krishnamurti, J. (1973), Education and Significance of Life, Krishnamurti Foundation, Varanasi.

Krishnamurti, J. (1997), The Flame of Attention, Krishnamurti Foundation Trust Ltd., London.

Kumar, K. (2007), Shanti Shiksha Aur Gandhi, Maharishi Valmiki College of Education, Delhi University, New Delhi.

Lawson, R.B., Goldstein, S.G. and Musty, R.E. (1975), Principal and Methods of Psychology, Oxford University Press, London.

Mangal, S.K. (2010), Statistics in Psychology and Education, PHI Learning Pvt. Ltd., New Delhi.

Maria, D. (2003), Trainer's Manual for Peace and Communal Harmony in the Classroom (compilation for private circulation). 11, Kalasagar, Mohanwadi, Yerawada, Pune.

Ministry of Human Resource Development (1993), Learning Without Burden: A Report of the Advisory Committee, (MHRD), Department of Education, New Delhi.

Montessori, Maria (1972), Education and Peace, Henry Regnery Company, Chicago.

Nagrath, R. (2010), Pieces to Peace, Diamond Pocket Books (P) Ltd., New Delhi.

Nalwa, V. (1992), The ABC of Research, Wiley Eastern Limited, New Delhi.

Narayan, S. (1994), Strategies for World Peace, Commonwealth Publisher, New Delhi.

National Curriculum Framework (2002), NCERT, New Delhi.

National Curriculum Framework (2005), NCERT, New Delhi.

National Curriculum Framework for Teacher Education (2009), NCTE, New Delhi.

NCERT (2006), Education for Peace, Position Paper of National Focus Group, NCERT, New Delhi.

New Era Development Institute (2002), Peace Education, Activities for Children - A Teacher's Guide. NEDI, Panchgani, India.

New Era Development Institute (2001), Educate These Children, A Teacher's Guide for Pre-primary Schools, Book Four: Peace Education, Character Education, Panchgani, India.

New Era Development Institute (2001), The Promotion of Unity and Concord: A Compilation of Statements from the World's Religions for Moral Education in Schools and Suggestions for Its Use, Panchgani, India.

New Era Development Institute (2002), Peace Education Activities for Children: A Teacher's Guide, Panchgani, India.

Pandey, S. (2004), Concept of Peace in 'Self-Instructional Package on Peace Education'. NCERT, New Delhi.

Pardesi, G. (1982), Contemporary Peace Research, Radiant Publisher, New Delhi.

Peace and Value Education for Schools Teachers Manual (2000), Publisher Dharma Bharati Hyderabad, A.P.

Radhakrishnan, S. (1933), East and West in Religion, George Allen and Unwin Ltd., London.

Ramchandran P. and Ramkumar V. (2007), Education in India, National Book Trust India, New Delhi.

Rayjada, B.S. and Verma, V. (2008), Shiksha Me Anusandhan Ke Avashyak Tatva, The Dimond Printing Press, Jaipur.

Report of National Policy on education, Govt. of India, (1986).

Report of the committee on religious and moral instructions (1960).

Report of the Education Commission, Govt. of India, (1964-66).

Report of the University Education Commission, Govt. of India, (1948-49).

Ruhela, S.P. (2000), Indian Society and Education in 2010, Indian Publishers' and Distributors, Delhi.

Rushdy, S. (2005), Living in Harmony: Teacher's Manual, Vol. I to VIII, Oxford University Press, New Delhi.

Sahi, J. (2000), Education and Peace, Akshar Mudra, Pune.

Samaddar, R. and Reifeld, H. (2001), Peace as Process, Manohar Publisher and Distributors, New Delhi.

Sarin, S. and Sarin, A. (2008), Shekshik Anusandhan Vidhiya, Vinod Pustak Mandir, Agra.

Sharma, R.K. and Sinha, R.K. (1996), Prospectives in Peace and Disarmament, Commonwealth Publisher, New Delhi.

Sharma, R.A.(2009), Shiksha Anusandhan, R Lal Book Depot, Meerut.

Sharma, R.N. (2007), Integral Thought of Sri Aurobindo, Shubhi Publications, Delhi.

Shrivastava, D.N. (1981), Anusandhan Vidhiya, Sahitya Prakashan, Agra.

Singh, M.K. and Kumar, A. (2007), Reading Gandhi, K.K. Publications, New Delhi.

Singh, R. (1998), The Gandhian Vision, Manak Publications (P) Limited, New Delhi.

Sukhiya, S.P. Mehrotra, P.V. and Mehrotra, R.N.(1981), Elements of Educational Research,Vinod Pustak Mandir, Agra.

Sumathi, S.(2005), Living in Harmony: A Course on Peace and Value Education. Book 1 to 8, Oxford University Press, New Delhi.

The Best of Speaking Tree (2002), A Times Group Presentation in Association with Diviniti, Bennett Coleman and Co. Ltd., New Delhi.

The Best of Speaking Tree (2002), A Times Group

Presentation in Association with Diviniti, Bennett Coleman and Co. Ltd., New Delhi.

The Hindu speaks on education (1997), Kasturi and Sons Limited, Chennai.

The Mother (1998), Health and Healing in Yoga, Selection from the writings and talks of Sri Aurobindo Ashram, Pondicherry.

The Universal House of Justice (1985), The Promise of World Peace (1985) Baha'i Publishing Trust, New Delhi.

Tillman, D. and Diana, H. (2000), Living Values Activities for Children Ages 3-7. Deerfield Beach, Health Communications, Inc., Florida.

Tillman, Diane (2000), Living Values Activities for Children Ages 8-14. Health Communications, Inc., Deerfield Beach, Florida.

Timpson, William M. (2002), Teaching and Learning Peace. Atwood Publishing, Madison, Wisconsin.

UNESCO (2002), Learning to Be: A Holistic and Integrated Approach to Value Education for Human Development, UNESCO, Bangkok.

UNESCO (2004), Learning to Live Together: Building Skills, Values and Attitudes for the Twenty First Century, UNESCO, New Delhi.

UNESCO (2005), Peace Education: Framework for Teacher Education, UNESCO, New Delhi.

Valson, T.(2006), Living in Harmony: A Course on Peace and Value Education, Oxford, New Delhi.

Vijay (2000), Meditation compiled from the writings of Sri Aurobindo and the Mother, Sri Aurobindo Society, Pondicherry.

Vyas R.N. (1987), Indian Wisdom and International Peace, Gian Publishing House, Delhi - 110007.

Journals and Theses

Adenike Yesufu (2000), Education for a Culture of Peace in Nigeria : The Role of a Womens Development NGO, Ph.D. , University of Alberta, Canada.

Anita L. Wenden (2007), Educating for a Critically Literate Civil Society: Incorporating the Linguistic Perspective into Peace Education, Journal of Peace Education, Routledge, London, Volume 4, Issue 2, pp. 163–180.

Bjerstedt, Ake (2003), Developing Preparedness for Peace: Objectives, Methods, Difficulties and Possibilities in Peace-Related Education. Peace Education Reports, Guides - Non-Classroom.

Bogart, Louise Berry (2000), A qualitative study of classroom culture in two elementary environments in which teachers who identify themselves as peace educators are implementing peace education practices with first grade children, Ph.D., University of Hawaii at Manoa.

Brantmeier, Edward J. (2003), Peace Pedagogy: Exposing and Integrating Peace Education in Teacher Education, Reports - Descriptive; Speeches/Meeting Papers.

Brown,Warren Donald (2000), School Children's perception of conflict : A view from the urban inner-city, Ph.D., Southeastern University, Manoa.

Candice C. Carter (2008),Voluntary Standards for Peace Education, Journal of Peace Education, Routledge, London, Volume 5, Issue 2 pp. 141–155.

Carl Christopher Mirra (2004), United States foreign policy since 1945 and the prospects for peace education, Ph.D., Columbia University, U.S.A.

Claire McGlynn (2004), Education for peace in integrated schools: a priority for Northern Ireland? Child Care in Practice, Routledge, London, Volume 10, Issue 2, pp. 85- 94.

E. M. Ajala (2007), The Impact of Relationship Management

of Peace Education on Labour-management Relations and Workers Welfare in Selected Industries in Nigeria, Department of Social Work, University of Ibadan, Ibadan, Nigeria.

Gavriel Salomon (2004), Does Peace Education Make a Difference in the Context of an Intractable Conflict? Peace and Conflict: Journal of Peace Psychology, Routledge, London, Volume 10, Issue 3, pp. 257- 274.

H.B. Danesh (2008), The Education for Peace integrative curriculum: concepts, contents and efficacy, Journal of Peace Education, Routledge, London,Volume 5, Issue 2, pp. 157- 173.

Hursh, Lydia Heidi (2001), A peace education study : Perceptation of U.S. adolescent women in international peace building camp, Ph.D., University of Denevar, Denevar.

Johnson, David W., Johnson, Roger T. (2005), Essential Components of Peace Education, Theory into Practice, Routledge, London, v44 n4 pp. 280-292.

Kupermintz, Haggai, Salomon Gavriel (2005), Lessons to Be Learned From Research on Peace Education in the Context of Intractable Conflict, Theory Into Practice, Routledge, London, v44 n4 pp. 293-302.

Macdonald, Lowerence (2003), Traditional approaches to citizenship education, globalization, towards a peace education framework, Ph.D., Dalhousie University, Canada.

Monisha Bajaj (2010), Conjectures on peace education and Gandhian studies: method, institutional development and globalization, Journal of Peace Education, Routledge, London, Volume 7, Issue 1, pp. 47-63.

Noam Schimmel (2009),Towards a sustainable and holistic model of peace education: a critique of conventional modes of peace education through dialogue in Israel, Journal of Peace Education, Routledge, London, Volume 6, Issue 1, pp. 51-68.

Pamela Bolotin Joseph, Leslie Smith Duss (2009), Teaching a pedagogy of peace: a study of peace educators in United States schools in the aftermath of September 11, Journal of Peace Education, Routledge, London, Volume 6, Issue 2, pp. 189-207.

Renat Shaykhutdinov (2010), Give peace a chance: Nonviolent protest and the creation of territorial autonomy arrangements, Journal of Peace Research, Sage, London, Vol. 47, No. 2, pp. 179-191.

Ruth Firer (2008), Virtual peace education, Journal of Peace Education, Routledge, London, Volume 5, Issue 2, pp. 193-207.

Sharma Rachnantika (2006), Developing a programme on peace education for prospective teachers, M.Ed. dissertation, MLS University, Udaipur.

Simon Harris, Nick Lewer (2005), Post-graduate peace education in Sri Lanka, Journal of Peace Education, Routledge, London, Volume 2, Issue 2, pp. 109-124.

Yaacov B. Yablon and Yaacov J. Katz (2001), Internet-Based Group Relations: A High School Peace Education Project in Israel, Educational Media International, Routledge, London, Volume 38, Issue 2 and 3, pp. 175-182.

Yaacov Boaz Yablon (2007), Cognitive rather than emotional modification in peace education programs: advantages and limitations, Journal of Moral Education, Routledge, London, Volume 36, Issue 1, pp. 51-65.

Yaacov Boaz Yablon (2009), Gender Differences in Peace Education programmes, Gender and Education, Routledge, London, Volume 21, Issue 6, pp. 689-701.

Research Surveys and Encyclopaedias

Buch M.B. (1974), A Survey of Research in Education, First Edition, M.S. University, Baroda.

Buch M.B.(1979), Second Survey of Research in Education (1972-78), M.S. University, Baroda.

Buch M.B. (1987), Third Survey of Research in Education (1978-83), NCERT, New Delhi.

Buch M.B. (1991), Fourth Survey of Research in Education (1983-88), Vol.1 and Vol. 2, NCERT, New Delhi.

Buch M.B. (1997), Fifth Survey of Research in Education (1988-92), Vol.1, NCERT, New Delhi.

Rajput J.S. (2004), Encyclopedia of Indian Education, Vol. II, L-Z, NCERT, New Delhi.

Sinha P.C. and Cherry K.(1996), International Encyclopedia of Peace, Security, Social Justice and Human Rights, Anmol Publications Pvt. Ltd., New Delhi.

Yadav N.S.(2006), Sixth Survey of Educational Research (1993-2000), Vol.1 and Vol. 2, NCERT, New Delhi.

Yadav R.S. and Mandal B.N. (2007), Global Encyclopedia of Education, Vol.1-4, Global Vision Publishing House, New Delhi.

Annexure

Annexure 1: BLUE PRINT

Max. Marks 60

Weightage to the objectives

S.No.	*Objective*	*No. of Question*	*Marks Allotted*	*Marks in Percentage*
1.	Knowledge	11	22	37
2.	Understanding	17	34	56
3.	Application	2	4	7
	Total	**30**	**60**	**100**

Weightage to the Course Content

S.No.	*Name of the Unit*	*No. of Question*	*Marks Allotted*	*Marks in Percentage*
1.	Peace Education – Need, importance and Meaning	8	16	27

2.	Human rights and fundamental rights according to constitution	4	8	13.33
3.	Fundamental duties according to constitution	4	8	13.33
4.	U.N. declaration on the rights of the child	4	8	13.34
5.	Disarmaments	3	6	10
6.	The behavioural pattern of prospective teachers and its implementation on peace education.	7	14	23
	Total	**30**	**60**	**100**

Weightage to objectives and course content

Unit / Objective	*Knowledge*	*Understanding*	*Application*	*Total*
1.	3(6)	4(8)	1(2)	8(16)
2.	1(2)	3(6)	–	4(8)
3.	2(4)	2(4)	–	4(8)
4.	2(4)	2(4)	–	4(8)
5.	2(4)	1(2)	–	3(6)
6.	1(2)	5(10)	1(2)	7(14)
Total	**11(22)**	**17(34)**	**2(4)**	**30(60)**

Marks are given in the bracket and total no. of questions are outside the bracket.

Annexure 2: Pre-and Post-Test

Note - The objectives of this test is to study the awareness for peace teaching among prospective teachers. You are requested to write the answers of each question on the sheet given to you. Write your answers without any hesitation and be true to yourself while answering. Each question carries two marks. Time provided for the test is one hour. If you have any doubt, make it clear with invigilator. Answers given by you will be used for research purpose only. Read questions carefully and answer within given time.

1. Give four reasons for providing teaching of peace education to prospective teachers.
2. Name four values which in your opinion are essential in the personality of teachers for peace education.
3. Name any four important festivals which should be organised in the school for the development of peace education in the minds and hearts of students.
4. Name four precautions to be taken while singing national anthem and national song.
5. Name four important values defined in the preamble of the Indian constitution.
6. What is the utility of peace education training programme for prospective teachers?

7. How can teachers of different subjects can use activities related to their subjects while teaching peace education to the students.
8. What is the name given by UNO to the decade -2000 to 2010?
9. What is the title given by the UNO to 2nd October, the birthday of Mahatma Gandhi ?
10. Name in which document the NCERT has proposed the peace education as a part of national curriculum.
11. Write your own definition for peace education.
12. Name the activities which you will like to organise in your classroom while teaching peace education.
13. Give four causes in support of including peace education in the curriculum of educational institutions.
14. Give four reasons in support of teaching peace education in the modern context.
15. Propose four practical activities for promoting peace education in educational institutes.
16. What is the name of international festival which is celebrated on 10th December in educational institutes?
17. Differentiate between human rights and fundamental duties.
18. Name the fundamental rights given to the citizens for defending violation of other fundamental rights.
19. The maintenance of peace is not possible in the absence of fundamental rights. Present two examples.
20. Name the constitutional amendment by which fundamental duties are included in the Indian constitution.
21. How many fundamental duties are given in Indian constitution? Name the article for the inclusion of fundamental duties.
22. Name the four values on which the freedom movement of India was fought.

23. Name any two project which can be taken in your institutions for protecting public properties.
24. When UNO declared the child rights?
25. Name any two reasons by which UNO included the child rights in its draft.
26. Suggests two child rights which should be given to the children by school and parents.
27. Give four examples of the violation of child rights by the teachers in educational institutions.
28. What are the two objectives behind disarmament movement?
29. Name the date, year and the places of Japan where atom bomb was droped during Second World War by America.
30. Name eight countries having atomic power.

Annexure 3: A Sample of One Unit of Teaching Package

UNIT - PEACE EDUCATION

(a) Concept of peace

(b) Peace education - meaning and importance

(c) Peace education - curriculum and objectives

(d) Content of peace education

(e) Peace education - teaching learning process

(f) Role of teacher for peace education

Specific objectives Knowledge

(a) Peace is an universal value. It means to raise the feeling to the highest context.

(b) Peaceful coexistence is the need of the hour.

(c) By teaching peace education one can bring peace culture in the social environment.

(d) Peace education is an activity based process.

Understanding

(a) The prospective teachers shall explain the concept of peace.

(b) They will present causes why peace education is essential.

(c) They will illustrate different examples of the activities for peace education.

(d) They will correlate peace education with the total development of personality.

Skill

(a) They will read and explain the chart presented on peace education.

(b) They will prepare charts regarding different activities related with peace education.

(c) They will collect different press notes on peace education and will discuss in the classroom.

Application

(a) They will submit different solutions on the issues related with violence, exploitations published in the newspapers.

Educational activities for teaching peace education

(a) Presenting stories, poems, important statements related with peace education.

(b) Discussion in the classroom on different aspect of peace education.

(c) Forming club and forums for spreading peace education.

(d) Interview with editors, press reporters and resource persons engaged in the activities of peace education.

Teaching learning activities

(a) Story telling.

(b) Arranging seminars and symposium.

(c) Preparing and exhibiting charts.

(d) Discussion on some items published in newspapers regarding peace education.

(e) Arranging debates and elocution competition on different topics of peace education.

Evaluation questions

(a) What do you mean by peace education.

(b) Present some examples of the personalities worked for promoting peace in the modern world.

(c) How we can build a peaceful world community.

(d) When a charter on peace and culture was presented in the general assembly of UNO.

(e) Which is the best and permanent way for promoting peace.

(f) What do you mean by peace education.

(g) Name the activities a teacher can organise for promoting peace education.

(h) Prepare a chart regarding different educational activities for promoting peace education.

Annexure 4: Interview Schedule

1. Is there any need to develop awareness about peace education among prospective teachers?
2. Will you promote peace education in your institute?
3. Is there any need to give knowledge, understanding and application about meaning, concept and techniques of peace education to our prospective teachers?
4. What values should be inculcated in our prospective teachers for developing peace education among their students?
5. Which methodology will you used for conducting peace education course?
6. What activities should be organised by teacher educators to promote peace education?
7. How teachers can use mass media in promoting peace education?
8. What should be the role of parent- teacher co-operation in developing peace education among students?
9. How teachers can spread peace culture while teaching their subject matter?

   (Depending interview, questions other than those included in the interview schedule may be asked as per the requirement of the situations.)

Annexure 5

Teaching Package

I N D E X

1. **इकाई – अ शांति शिक्षा**
   1. शांति की अवधारणा
   2. शांति शिक्षा – अर्थ एवं महत्व
   3. शांति शिक्षा – पाठ्यक्रम एवं उद्देश्य
   4. शांति शिक्षा से सम्बधित विषय एंव विषयवस्तु
   5. शांति शिक्षा की शिक्षण प्रक्रिया एंव क्रियाऐं
   6. शांति शिक्षा के लिए अध्यापक की भूमिका
2. **इकाई – ब मानव अधिकार एवं मौलिक अधिकार**
   1. मानव अधिकार की अवधारणा
   2. मानव अधिकार की सार्वभौम घोषणा
   3. प्रमुख मानव अधिकार
   4. भारतीय संविधान में मौलिक अधिकार

3. इकाई – स भारतीय संविधान में मौलिक दायित्व

1. मौलिक अधिकारों की पृष्ठभूमि एवं प्रथम पांच मौलिक दायित्व
2. मौलिक दायित्व छः से दस एवं उनकी उपयोगिता

4. इकाई – द संयुक्त राष्ट्र संघ द्वारा घोषित बाल अधिकार

1. बाल अधिकार (पृष्ठभूमि, आवश्यकता, महत्व, संप्रत्यय)
2. संयुक्त राष्ट्रसंध द्वारा धोषित प्रमुख बाल अधिकार

5. इकाई–य शांति शिक्षा के भावी सक्रियतावादी अध्यापक का व्यवहारगत स्वरूप

1. भावी अध्यापक
2. शांति शिक्षा के अध्यापक
3. शांति शिक्षा के सक्रियतावादी अध्यापक का व्यवहारगत स्वरूप
4. शांति शिक्षा के भावी सक्रियतावादी अध्यापक की भूमिका

6. इकाई – र शांति शिक्षा एवं निःशस्त्रीकरण

1. आवश्यकता एवं महत्व
2. निःशस्त्रीकरण का अर्थ
3. निःशस्त्रीकरण एवं उस हेतु किये गये प्रयत्न
4. U.N.O. के निःशस्त्रीकरण हेतु किये गये प्रयास
5. निःशस्त्रीकरण के प्रयास एवं अध्यापक की भूमिका

शांति पाठ शैक्षणिक परियोजना के संप्रत्यय की भूमिका

Conceptual Introduction to the Peace Lessons (Teaching Package)

प्रस्तुत शांति पाठों से सम्बन्धित शैक्षणिक परियोजना (Teaching Package) का उद्देश्य भावी छात्राध्यापिकाओं के मन में स्वतंत्रता समानता एंव बन्धुत्व के भाव जाग्रत कर शांतिपूर्ण जीवन व्यतीत करने के लिए प्रेरित करना है।

शांति पाठों के अन्तर्ग्रत उन इकाईयों को लिया गया है जिनके ज्ञान एवं अभिबोध द्वारा छात्राध्यापिकाऐं अपनें व्यक्तिगत एवं सामाजिक जीवन में आने वाले संघर्षो का निवारण शांतिपूर्ण एवं लोकतंत्रीय तरीकों से कर सकें। इनका एक प्रमुख उद्वेश्य मानव मन एवं मस्तिष्क से युद्व. हिंसा एवं धृणा के भाव का अन्त कर इनसें शांति सद्भावना एवं मैत्री के भाव जाग्रत करना भी है। इन पाठों की परियोजना में उन विभिन्न शैक्षणिक क्रियाकलापों को लिया गया है जो उनकें चिन्तन एवं विचार विर्मश को प्रभावित कर शांति के एवं बंधुत्व के प्रति आस्था के भाव उत्पन्न करते है ।

शोधार्थी को आाशा है कि इन पाठों के शिक्षण के उपरान्त भावी छात्राध्यापिकाऐं शांति शिक्षक (Peace educators) की भूमिका का निर्वहन कर सकेगी।

इकाई अ – शान्ति शिक्षा

Peace Education

उपइकाई :–

1. शांति की अवधारणा
2. शांति शिक्षा – अर्थ एवं महत्व
3. शांति शिक्षा – पाठ्यक्रम एवं उद्वेश्य
4. शांति शिक्षा से सम्बधित विषय एंव विषयवस्तु
5. शांति शिक्षा की शिक्षण प्रक्रिया एंव क्रियाऐं
6. शांति शिक्षा के लिए अध्यापक की भूमिका

विशिष्ठ उद्वेश्य :–

ज्ञान :–

स्नातक अध्यापक इस पाठ को पढ़ाने के उपरान्त निम्नाकिंत तथ्यों का प्रत्यास्मरण एवं पुर्न पहचान कर सकेंगे।

1. शांति सत्य एवं प्रेम की तरह ही आवश्यक सार्वभौमिक मूल्य हैं शांति का अर्थ व्यक्ति की चेतना की भावना को उच्च चेतना तक उठाने से है।
2. शांतिपूर्ण सह अस्तित्व आज के विश्व की सर्वोपरि आवश्यकता है।
3. शांति शिक्षा के माध्यम से व्यक्तिगत से लेकर सामाजिक स्तर तक वर्तमान वातावरण में शांतिभाव की स्थापना की जा सकती है।

4. शांति शिक्षा एक उद्वेश्य पूर्ण प्रक्रिया है।

अवबोध :–

1. भावी अध्यापक शांति एवं शांति शिक्षा की अवधारणा की व्याख्या कर सकेंगे।
2. शांति एवं शांति शिक्षा व्यक्ति के लिये क्यों आवश्यक है। इसके कारण बता सकेंगे।
3. शांति शिक्षा हेतु अध्यापक द्वारा की जाने वाली विभिन्न शैक्षिक क्रियाओं के उदाहरण दे सकेंगे।
4. शांति शिक्षा का मानव व्यक्तित्व के सर्वांगीण विकास से सबंध स्थापित कर करेंगे।

कौशल :–

1. भावी अध्यापक शांति शिक्षा के उद्वेश्यों को चार्ट में पढ़ाकर उनकी व्याख्या करेंगे।
2. भावी अध्यापक शांति शिक्षा से सम्बन्धित विविध क्रियाओं का वर्गीकरण कर उनसे सम्बन्धित चार्ट का निर्माण करेंगे।
3. शांति शिक्षा से सम्बन्धित प्रेस विज्ञप्ति एकत्रित कर कक्षा में उस पर परिचर्चा कर सकेंगे।

ज्ञानोपयोग :–

समाचार पत्रों में से हिंसा शोषण आदि घटनाओं का प्रस्तुतिकरण करने पर छात्राध्यापक उनके समाधान के विविध विकल्पों में से सही विकल्प संबन्धित निर्णय ले सकेंगे।

पाठ्यवस्तु विश्लेषण –

शांति की अवधारण :–

शांति–प्रेम, सत्य, शुद्धता (मन, वचन एवं कर्म), सुन्दरता, प्रकृति के साथ समन्वय, उत्तरदायित्व के प्रति जागरूकता, अहिंसा, मानवता, सकारात्मक सोच एंव आत्मनियंत्रण की तरह ही एक सार्वभौमिक मूल्य हैं। व्यक्तित्व निर्माण के लिये समाज राष्ट्र एवं विश्व को जिन आवश्यक मूल्यों की स्थापना करने की आवश्यकता होती है वे सब परस्पर आपस में जुड़े हुए हैं एवं इनमें से किसी भी एक को अलग कर विकास की कल्पना नहीं की जा सकती है।

शांति सत्य व प्रेम की तरह ही आवश्यक सार्वभौमिक मूल्य है और इसकी प्राप्ति के बिना अन्य मूल्यों की स्थापना के बारे में नहीं सोचा जा सकता हैं। शांति का अर्थ मतभेद एंव रूचियों में अन्तर समाप्त करना नहीं है। प्रत्येक मानव वैयक्तित्व विभिन्नता का केन्द्र हैं और अपनी व्यक्तिगत सोच सत्य उसके साथ रहता है। शांतिपूर्ण समाज में विविध अन्तर एवं मतभेदों को परस्पर विचारविमर्श एवं बातचीत द्वारा एक दूसरे की भावनाओं का सम्मान करते हुए परस्पर सुलझाव द्वारा दूर किया जाता है। आर्थिक, सामाजिक, बौद्धिक एवं नैतिक मानवीय विकास शांति की रीढ़ है। वास्तविक विकसित समाज में प्रत्येक की मूलभूत आवश्यकता भोजन, कपड़ा, मकान, स्वास्थ्य, शिक्षा, सुरक्षा, आत्मसम्मान और एक दूसरे के प्रति सम्मान को बनाये रखा जाता है। जाति, धर्म, सम्प्रदाय एवं जन्म के आधार पर कोई अन्तर नहीं किया जाता है। ऊंच–नीच की भावना का कोई स्थान नहीं होता है। सभी व्यक्तियों में एकता की भावना होती है।

शांति का अर्थ व्यक्ति की चेतना की भावना को उच्च चेतना तक उठाने से है। जैसे जैसे व्यक्ति इस अवस्थाओं को प्राप्त करता जायेगा वह शांति के नजदीक होगा। बुद्ध, ईसा, महावीर, मोहम्मद साहब, महात्मा गांधी आदि शांति के प्रणेता थे और मानवीय विकास में इन्होंने अपना बहुमूल्य योगदान दिया। शांति के लिये शिक्षा का व्यक्तियों को इसी पथ पर आगे बढ़ाने की बात करती

है। शांतिमय विश्व ही एक पूर्ण विश्व हो सकता है। हम इसकी निर्माण योजना में कितने सचेत है? यह एक दो दिन का कार्य नहीं है वरन् इस पर निर्भर करता है कि हम कितना कार्य अधिकाधिक एकता स्थापना, प्रेम एवं मूल्य स्थापना हेतु कर रहे हैं और इसी आधार पर अधिक शांति हमारे परिवार में, हमारे विधालयों में हमारे पड़ोस में, समाज में तथा हमारे गांव, शहर, राज्य, राष्ट्र एवं सम्पूर्ण विश्व में आ सकती है।

शांति शिक्षा की अवधारणा :–

''विश्व के राष्ट्रों में शांति एवं सद्भावना के विकास हेतु भारत सदैव प्रयत्नशील रहा है और ऐसी संस्कृति शिक्षा द्वारा ही विकसित की जा सकती है। शिक्षा ही अन्तर्राष्ट्रीय शांति एवं सद्भाव छात्रों में जागृत कर सकती है। शांतिपूर्ण सह अस्तित्व आज के विश्व की सर्वोपरि आवश्यकता है जिसकी अवहेलना कदापि नहीं की जा सकती है।'' (राष्ट्रीय शिक्षा नीति 1986 एम. एच. आर. डी. 1992, पृष्ठ 6)

आज का विश्व अशांति, हिंसा एवं युद्ध की ज्वाला में धधक रहा है। विश्व में शांति की स्थापना एवं मानव मन को शांत व तनाव रहित बनाना आज की महती आवश्यकता है। विगत कुछ समय से शैक्षिक जगत में ''शांति शिक्षा'' पर पर्याप्त विचार विमर्श एवं मंथन चल रहा है। 1999 की संयुक्त राष्ट्र संघ की साधारण सभा ने संस्कृति और शांति आधारित एक घोषणा पत्र पारित किया जिसमें प्रतिदिन के जीवन व्यवहार में शांति के महत्व को एवं उसके लिये की जाने वाली शैक्षिक क्रियाओं की प्रस्तुती की गयी है।

भारत में भी राष्ट्रीय एवं भावनात्मक एकता खण्डित हो रही है। समाजिक व आर्थिक असमानता तेजी से बढ़ने के साथ ही हमारी बहुलवादी संस्कृति और अहिसंक परम्परा पर खतरे मंडरा

रहे है। हिंसा का साम्राज्य परिवार और समाज में सर उठाकर मानव शांति की आधारशिला को सरका रहा है। आज के इस वातावरण में शांति भाव की स्थापना व्यक्तिगत स्तर से लेकर सामाजिक स्तर तक प्रभावपूर्ण तरीके से लायी जानी आवश्यक है। इस उद्देश्य की प्राप्ति शिक्षा के माध्यम से ही प्रभावपूर्ण एवं स्थायी रूप से प्राप्त की जा सकती है।

राष्ट्रीय शैक्षिक अनुसंधान और प्रशिक्षण परिषद ने राष्ट्रीय पाठ्यचर्या की रूपरेखा (एन.सी.एफ.) 2005 में भी शांति की शिक्षा की पुरजोर वकालत की है तथा उसे पाठ्यक्रम का अंग बनाने एवं उसके लिए अध्यापक शिक्षा में भी कार्यक्रम बनाने पर जोर दिया है। शांति शिक्षा शिक्षा जगत में एक नयी पहल के रूप में उभर रहा है।

शांति शिक्षा की विभिन्न परिभाषाएं :–

शांति शिक्षा को कई शिक्षाविदों ने अर्थ देने का प्रयास किया है इनमें से कुछ निम्नानुसार है–

थेम्पो वेलसन, एन. सी. ई. आर. टी. सेमिनार 2004–

''शांतिपूर्ण वातावरण के निर्माण हेतु जिस ज्ञान, कौशल, अभिवृत्तियों एवं मूल्यों की आवश्यकता है उन्हें सृजन करने वाली प्रक्रिया ही शांति शिक्षा है। यह शांतिपरक व्यक्तियों के निर्माण एवं संघर्षो को अहिंसात्मक रूप से सुलझाने वाली प्रक्रिया भी है।''

एन.सी.ई.आर.टी. द्वारा प्रस्तुत नेशनल क्युरीकुलम फ्रेमवर्क –

''शांति शिक्षा ऐसी नैतिक चेतना का विकास है जिसमें उन मूल्यों, अभिवृत्तियों एवं कुशलताओं का निर्माण किया जाता है जो आनन्ददायी व्यक्तिगत एवं सामाजिक जीवन जीने की कला को विकसित करती है। यह जीवन कला आनन्द एवं उच्च कोटि के स्नेह, आशा एवं उत्साह को प्रदर्शित करता है। ऐसे जीवन में

मानव अधिकार, न्याय, सहिष्णुता, सहयोग, सामाजिक दायित्व एवं बहुलवादी संस्कृति को आदर एवं जनतंत्रीय स्वरूप के प्रति आस्था का भाव होता है। ऐसे जीवन में अहिंसक तरीके से समस्याओं का समाधान किया जाता है तथा यहाँ सामाजिक न्याय सर्वसुलभ होता है।''

शांति शिक्षा का सर्वमान्य अर्थ

शांति शिक्षा से सम्बन्धित विभिन्न सम्प्रत्ययों पर विचार कर शांति शिक्षा का जो एक सर्वमान्य अर्थ निकलता है उसे निम्नानुसार व्यक्त किया जा सकता है –

1 शांति शिक्षा एक नैतिक चेतना का विकास है।

2 यह छात्रों में शांतिपूर्ण विश्व के निर्माण हेतु ज्ञान, कौशल एवं अभिवृत्तियों को विकसित करने की शैक्षिक प्रक्रिया है।

3 यह भावी विश्व के जीवन में आनन्द सृजित करने एवं मानव अधिकार, न्याय, सहिष्णुता, सहयोग एवं बहुलवादी विश्व संस्कृति की स्थापना में सहायक है।

शांति शिक्षा का महत्व –

हम अभूतपूर्व हिंसा के दौर में जी रहे है। इस दौर में असहिष्णुता, कट्टरवाद, विवाद की निरन्तर आशंकाए है। अनसुलझे विवादों से युद्व एवं हिंसा पैदा होती है। आज आवश्यकता इस बात की है कि हिंसा का यह दौर समाप्त हो और आपसी विवादों को अहिंसात्मक तरीके से निपटाया जाये। शांति की शिक्षा द्वारा यह सम्भव है।

शांति शिक्षा द्वारा व्यक्ति में सहनशीलता, न्याय, अन्तःसांस्कृतिक समझ और नागरिक दायित्वों की पालना का भाव उत्पन्न होता है अतः एक लोकतांत्रिक समाज एवं लोकतांत्रिक मूल्यों से परिपूर्ण

नागरिकों को तैयार करने में शांति शिक्षा का बडा महत्व है।

शांति शिक्षा मूल्य परख शिक्षा का मार्ग प्रशस्त करती है। पाठ्यक्रम के सभी विषयों और सभी पाठों में कोई न कोई मूल्य जुड़े होते है। शांति शिक्षा के माध्यम से अध्यापक में यह जागरूकता उत्पन्न होती है कि वह प्रत्येक विषय एवं प्रत्येक पाठ को पढ़ाते समय उनमें अन्तःर्निहित मूल्यों को छात्रों के सामने उजागर करें।

शांति शिक्षा व्यक्ति में प्रकृति और मानव जगत के बीच सामन्जस्य बिठानें मे मदद करती है। शांति शिक्षा द्वारा व्यक्ति के मन में हर्ष , प्रेम, न्याय, सहिष्णुता, सहकार, सामाजिक दायित्व, सांस्कृतिक विविधता का सम्मान करना आदि अनेक मूल्यें का जागरण होता है जो उसे जीवन एवं प्रकृति के साथ सामन्जस्य बिठानें में मदद करते है।

शांति शिक्षा का महत्व इस रूप में भी है कि वह समस्त विद्यालय जीवन, पाठ्यचर्या, कक्षा वातावरण, स्कूल प्रबन्धन, शिक्षक विद्यार्थी सम्बन्ध आदि तमाम गतिविधियों से जुडी हुई है। शांति शिक्षा द्वारा आपसी पर्यावरण एवं मीडिया द्वारा प्रचारित हिंसा के भाव जो बच्चों के मन को प्रभावित करते है उन्हें दूर करने में भी सहायता मिलती है।

शांति शिक्षा में बच्चों को हिंसा के स्थान पर शांति के लिए प्रेरित किया जाता है। शांति शिक्षा के शिक्षण द्वारा भावी अध्यापकों को शांति शिक्षा का सक्रिय वाहक (Peace Education Activitist) बनाया जा सकता है।

शांति शिक्षा का पाठ्यक्रम –

शांति शिक्षा के अर्थ को दृष्टिगत रखते हुए यदि इसके लागू करने की बात की जाये तो शांति शिक्षा को पाठय्क्रम में व्यापक

रूप से लिया जाना चाहिये तथा उसका अधिकांश रूप व्यावहारिक एवं वातावरण सृजित होना चाहिए।

वर्तमान समय में हिंसा, अशांति और संघर्ष के विकराल स्वरूप को देखते हुए शांति शिक्षा के केवल सैद्वांतिक पाठ्यक्रम को लागू कर देना ही अपरिहार्य ही नहीं होगा वरन् यह आवश्यक है कि शांति शिक्षा के अंतर्गत अनुभविक क्रियाओं को विशेष महत्व दिया जाये। अनुभविक रूप से सीखी गयी विषय वस्तु स्मृति में अधिक समय तक बनी रहती है। वर्तमान समय में अनुभविक क्रियाओं पर बल देकर न सिर्फ पाठ्यक्रम का बोझ कम हो सकेगा वरन् विद्यार्थियों के मानसपटल पर शांति पाठ को स्थायी रूप से अंकित कर ऐसे नागरिकों का निर्माण किया जा सकेगा जो विश्व में शांति, सौहार्द तथा सद्भाव कायम कर इस विश्व को विकास की नयी दिशाऐं प्रदान कर सकेंगे।

शांति शिक्षा के उद्देश्य

शांति शिक्षा के उद्देश्य भावी शिक्षकों के लिए निम्नाकिंत हैं –

1 शांति शिक्षा का उद्देश्य विश्व में शांति की स्थापना करने वाली शांति संस्कृति के सृजन हेतु तन्मयता से कार्य करने वाले व्यक्तित्वों का निर्माण करना है।

2 इसका उद्देश्य छात्रों के व्यक्तित्व में उन मूल्यों का सृजन करना है जो समाज में शांतिमय वातावरण निर्मित करने में सहायक हो सके। शांति शिक्षा छात्रों को ऐसी जीवन जीने की कला सिखाना एवं ऐसी जीवन पद्धति का निर्माण करना है जो शांतिमय समाज की स्थापना कर सके।

3 इसका उद्देश्य छात्रों को ऐसे सहभागिता पूर्ण जीवन जीने की कला में प्रशिक्षित करना है जिससे वे एक उत्तम एवं उदारवादी नागरिक बन सकें।

शांति शिक्षा संबन्धित विषय एवं विषयवस्तु :–

शांति शिक्षा के अन्तर्गत महत्वपूर्ण विषय के रूप में कला, संगीत, खेलकूद, उद्योग, योग एवं ध्यान, नृत्य, तुलनात्मक धार्मिक शिक्षा, नैतिक शिक्षा, साहित्यिक विषय, इतिहास, नागरिक शास्त्र, मानविकी एवं सामाजिक विज्ञान विषयों में शांति शिक्षा के अर्न्तगत विश्व के महान धर्मो का तुलनात्मक अध्ययन एवं जन सेवा के उदाहरणों को शामिल किया जाना चाहिए। शांति शिक्षा में खेलकूद संबंधित स्वस्थ रूचियों के सृजन एवं नागरिक दायित्व के प्रति जागरूकता के भाव को प्रमुखता दी जानी चाहिए।

शांति शिक्षा की शिक्षण प्रक्रिया:–

भावी शिक्षक शांति शिक्षा की शिक्षण प्रक्रिया में अपना महत्वपूर्ण योगदान किस प्रकार दे सकते है जिससे कि वे समाज में शांतिभाव की स्थापना अपने विद्यार्थियों के माध्यम से कर सकें और सम्पूर्ण राष्ट्र एवं एकल विश्व गांव के निर्माण में अपनी महत्वपूर्ण भूमिका का उचित प्रकार से निर्वहन कर सके यह एक महत्वपूर्ण प्रश्न है।

शांति शिक्षा की प्रक्रिया में आपसी विचार विमर्श एवं वाद–विवाद पद्धति प्रभावी भूमिका निभा सकते है। कक्षा शिक्षण में भी शांति शिक्षा के लिये वाद विवाद, संवाद, विचार विमर्श, प्रभावशाली माध्यम सिद्ध हो सकते हैं। 1999 के संयुक्त राष्ट्र संघ की साधारण सभा द्वारा प्रस्तुत घोषणापत्र में समस्या समाधान विधि, संप्रेषण विधि, ध्यान विधि, शांतिपूर्ण जीवन व्यवहार एवं सहयोग की क्रियाओं को अपनाने की बात कही गयी है। एन. सी. ई. आर. टी. द्वारा प्रस्तुत नेशनल क्युरीकुलम फ्रेमवर्क के अनुसार "शांतिभाव की शिक्षा का समावेश सम्पूर्ण शैक्षिक प्रक्रिया में अन्तर्निहित होना चाहिये इसकी झलक सम्पूर्ण विद्यालय जीवन एवं उसकी पाठ्यक्रमिक क्रियाओं, पाठ्य सहगामी क्रियाओं, कक्षा वातावरण, विद्यालय प्रबन्ध, छात्र अध्यापक सम्बन्ध, अध्ययन अधिगम प्रक्रिया एवं विद्यालय के समस्त कार्यक्रमों में मिलनी चाहिये।"

इस हेतु शांति शिक्षा के लिए पाठ्य सहगामी क्रियाओं एवं विविध शैक्षिक क्रियाओं की आयोजना करना आवश्यक है। शांति शिक्षा की शिक्षण व्यूह रचना के लिये एक विधि निर्धारित नहीं की जा सकती हैं। जिस भी शिक्षण विधि का चयन किया जाये वह अनुभव आधारित, क्रिया आधारित एवं छात्र केन्द्रित होनी चाहिये। प्रश्नोत्तरी, कहानी, नाटक, पर्यटन भी शांति शिक्षा में महत्वपूर्ण भूमिका निभा सकते है। प्राइमरी क़क्षाओं में विविध खेलों द्वारा शांति भाव की शिक्षा दी जा सकती है।

शांति शिक्षा कार्यक्रम के अर्न्तगत ली जाने वाली शैक्षिक क्रियाएँ –

शांति शिक्षा कार्यकम के उद्देश्यों की सफलता हेतु निम्नांकित शैक्षिक कियाऐं आयोजित की जानी चाहिये–

1. हमारे प्राचीन श्रेष्ठ शिक्षक कहानियों एवं लोकोक्तियों को नैतिकता व सामाजिक संदेश देने का श्रेष्ठ माध्यम समझते थे। शांति भाव के जागरण हेतु शिक्षक कहानियों व लोकोक्तियों को शिक्षा का माध्यम बना सकता है।

2. कक्षा में अध्यापक द्वारा विविध विषयों पर छात्रों को अपने विचार रखने एवं विचार विमर्श में भाग लेने को प्रोत्साहित किया जाना चाहिए। विद्यालयों में ऐसे क्लब एवं वाचनालयों की व्यवस्था की जाये जहाँ शांति भाव को बढ़ावा देने वाली घटनाओं और सूचनाओं के संग्रहण व अध्ययन की सुविधा हो।

3. शांतिभाव को बढ़ावा देने वाले चलचित्रों, टी.वी. एवं आकाशवाणी के सीरियल्स एवं विविध कार्यक्रमों की सूची तैयार करना एवं उनके प्रसारण का प्रबन्ध करना।

4. सूचना प्रसारण से सम्बन्धित विविध अभिकरणों से संवाददाता, संपादक एवं ऐसे सन्दर्भ व्यक्तियों को

शिक्षण संस्थाओं में आमंत्रित किया जाय इस विषय पर विद्यार्थियों का ज्ञान बढ़ाने एवं उनके सुझावों का प्रकाशन व प्रसारण का कार्य करें।

5. शिक्षण संस्थाओं में भारत की बहुलवादी एवं विविध धार्मिक संस्कृति से सम्बन्धित उत्सव एवं पर्वों की आयोजना सोल्लास की जाये।

6. विद्यालयों में महिलाओं के प्रति आदरभाव की अभिवृत्ति के विकास हेतु विभिन्न कार्यक्रमों की आयोजना की जाये।

शांति शिक्षा के लिए अध्यापक की भूमिका –

शांति शिक्षा का कार्य प्रभावी रूप से वे समर्पित शिक्षक ही कर सकते है जो शांति पूर्ण वातावरण के निर्माता एवं उनके संरक्षणकर्ता हों। महान विश्व शिक्षक कृष्णमूर्ति के अनुसार "एक जीवन्त और शांतिपूर्ण समाज के निर्माण की आधारशिला रखने का मुख्य दायित्व अध्यापक का ही है। हम बच्चों को शिक्षा इसलिये देते हैं कि वे आत्मज्ञान की और बढ़ें, जिसके बिना न तो जीवन में शांति संभव है और न आनन्द। अध्यापक को छात्रों के साथ सहज सम्बन्ध बनाते हुए शांति भाव की शिक्षा प्रदान करना चाहिये। शिक्षक को स्वयं को सबसे पहले नये सिरे से शिक्षित होना चाहिये।

छात्रों से सम्पर्क के विविध अवसरों पर अध्यापकों को उनके आत्मविश्वास बढानें में मदद करनी चाहिये एवं कटु व हिंसात्मक विचारों व प्रवृतियों से छात्रों को दूर रखने का प्रयास करना चाहिये।

शिक्षकों को शिक्षण प्रक्रिया में ऐसी शैक्षणिक क्रियाओं का आयोजन करना चाहिए जो उनमें सकारात्मक विचार, अपने अनुभवों से कुछ खोजने, प्रयोग करने, निर्माण करने, निर्णय लेने की क्षमता

विकसित करें जिससे छात्रों में शांतिभाव सम्बन्धित मूल्य विकसित हो सके।

गांधी जी के विचारों के अनुसार यह कह सकते हैं कि "यह शिक्षा स्वयं में पूर्ण समन्वित एवं जिस समाज में हम रह रहे हैं उसके लिये उपयोगी एवं सार्थक शैक्षिक प्रक्रिया है।"

अध्ययन अध्यापन क्रियाऐं :–

1. शांति शिक्षा से सम्बन्धित कहानी को विषय शिक्षण में प्रयुक्त किया जायेगा।
2. शांति शिक्षा के अर्थ एवं महत्व को स्पष्ट करने हेतु परिचर्चा की आयोजना की जायेगी।
3. शांति शिक्षा के लिये की जाने वाली क्रियाओं का चार्ट प्रदर्शित किया जायेगा।
4. समाचार पत्रों में प्रकाशित शांति समाप्त करने वाली घटनाओं को प्रस्तुत कर उन पर परिचर्चा की जायेगी।
5. विद्यालयों को किन किन क्रियाओं के माध्यम से शांति स्थापित की जा सकती है के बारे में छात्रों के मध्य समूह चर्चा की जायेगी।
6. शांति शिक्षा से सम्बन्धित वाद विवाद प्रतियोगिता की आयोजना की जायेगी।

मूल्याकंन प्रश्न :–

1. शांति का क्या अर्थ है?
2. शांति के प्रणेता व्यक्तियों के नाम बताइए?
3. शांति की अवस्था में ऊँच नीच की भावना का क्या स्थान होता है?

4. शांतिपूर्ण विश्व का निर्माण किस प्रकार किया जा सकता है?
5. संयुक्त राष्ट्र संघ की साधारण सभा ने संस्कृति और शांति आधारित घोषणा पत्र कब पारित किया?
6. शांतिभाव स्थापना की प्राप्ति का सबसे प्रभावी एवं स्थायी माध्यम कौनसा है?
7. शांति शिक्षा का क्या अर्थ है?
8. शांति शिक्षा द्वारा कैसे नागरिकों का निर्माण किया जा सकता है?
9. शांति शिक्षा हेतु अध्यापक कौन कौनसी शैक्षिक क्रियाऐं आयोजित कर सकता है?
10. अपने विद्यार्थियों को शांति प्रिय नागरिक बनाने के लिए आप अपने विद्यालय में किन किन क्रियाओं की आयोजना करेंगे?
11. शांति शिक्षा हेतु अपनायी जाने वाली प्रमुख क्रियाओं को एक चार्ट रूप में प्रदर्शित कीजिये।

इकाई ब – मानव अधिकार एवं मौलिक अधिकार

Human Rights and Fundamental Rights

उपइकाई :–

1. मानव अधिकार की अवधारणा
2. मानव अधिकार की सार्वभौम घोषणा
3. प्रमुख मानव अधिकार
4. भारतीय संविधान में मौलिक अधिकार

विशिष्ट उद्देश्य :–

ज्ञान –

स्नातक अध्यापक इस पाठ के पढ़ाने के उपरान्त निम्नांकित तथ्यों का पुनःस्मरण एवं पुनः पहचान कर सकेंगे।

1. मानव अधिकार समस्त मानव जाति के जन्म सिद्ध अधिकार है तथा उसके व्यक्तित्व के सर्वांगीण विकास के लिये आवश्यक है।
2. संयुक्त राष्ट्र संघ ने 10 दिसम्बर 1948 को मानवाधिकारों की सार्वभौमिक घोषणा की।
3. स्वतंत्रता, समानता, न्यायप्राप्ति मुख्य मौलिक अधिकार है।
4. इन अधिकारों में सामाजिक, आर्थिक राजनैतिक, धार्मिक सांस्कृतिक, विविध प्रकार के अधिकारों को शामिल किया गया है।
5. इनसे प्रेरणा प्राप्त कर विविध देशों के संविधानो में इन्हें कानूनी मान्यता प्रदान की गयी है?
6. भारतीय संविधान में भी नागरिकों को प्रमुख छः मौलिक अधिकार प्रदान किये गये है। ये सभी अधिकार कानूनी मान्यता प्राप्त है। कोई भी नागरिक इनका उल्लंघन होने पर न्यायिक शरण में जा सकता है तथा अपराधी को समूचित दण्ड दिया जा सकता है।
7. इन अधिकारों के ज्ञान एवं उनकी अनुपालना द्वारा मानव जीवन मं शांति और समाज में भी शांति एवं सद्भाव की स्थापना की जा सकती है।

अवबोध –

1. मानव अधिकारों की अवधारणा अथवा परिभाषा की

व्याख्या कर सकेंगे।

2. मानव अधिकारों और मौलिक अधिकारों में अन्तर कर सकेंगे।
3. मौलिक अधिकार व्यक्ति के लिये क्यों आवश्यक है इसके लिये कारण बता सकेंगे।
4. विविध प्रकार के मौलिक अधिकारों के उदाहरण प्रस्तुत कर सकेंगे।
5. व्यक्ति ओर समाज के जीवन की शांति का मौलिक अधिकारों के साथ सम्बन्ध स्थापित कर सकेंगे।

कौशल –

1. मौलिक अधिकारों का चार्ट बना सकेंगे।
2. विद्यालय बुलेटिन बोर्ड पर पिछले कुछ दिनों में मानव अधिकारों के उल्लंघन से सम्बन्धित घटनाओं की प्रेस विज्ञप्ति प्रदर्शित कर सकेंगे।
3. मानव अधिकारों के बढ़ते हुए उल्लंघंन से सम्बन्धित घटनाओं पर समाचार पत्र के सम्पादक के नाम पत्र लिख सकेंगे।

ज्ञानोपयोग –

1. मानव अधिकार उल्लंघन से सम्बन्धित किसी घटना के सम्बन्ध में उठाये जाने वाले उपायों से सम्बन्धित निर्णय ले सकेंगे।

पाठ्यवस्तु विश्लेषण –

1 मानव अधिकार की अवधारणा –

प्रत्येक व्यक्ति के व्यक्तित्व के विकास के लिए उसे कुछ

अवसर प्राप्त होने आवश्यक है जिन्हें हम मानव की जन्मजात आवश्यकताएं भी कह सकते है, जिनके अभाव में वह व्यक्ति अपने जीवन को सुखी और सुरक्षित नहीं रख सकता है। जैसे अपने विचार व्यक्त करने का अवसर बिना भेदभाव के अपनी योग्यता के अनुरूप नौकरी प्राप्त करने का अवसर, किसी स्थान पर आने जाने और बसने का अवसर, बिना किसी भेदभाव के न्याय पाने का अवसर आदि। मानव की इन्हीं जन्मजात आवश्यकताओं या अवसर प्राप्ति को विद्वतजनों ने मानव अधिकार का नाम दिया है जिसे प्रत्येक समाज और सरकार द्वारा प्रदान किया जाता है।

2 मानव अधिकार की सार्वभौम घोषणा –

10 दिसम्बर, 1948 को संयुक्त राष्ट्र संघ की जनरल एसेम्बली ने मानव अधिकारों की सार्वभौम घोषणा को स्वीकृति प्रदान की तब से प्रति वर्ष 10 दिसम्बर का दिन मानव अधिकार दिवस के रूप में सारे विश्व में मनाया जाता है।

3 प्रमुख मानव अधिकार –

संयुक्त राष्ट्र संघ के घोषणा पत्र में 30 अनुच्छेद है जिनमें मानव अधिकारों का वर्णन किया गया है इनमें प्रमुख निम्नाकिंत है–

1. प्रत्येक मानव को जन्मजात स्वंत्रता और समानता प्राप्त है अतः उन्हें भाई–चारे के भाव से रहना चाहिये।
2. समस्त मानवों को यह अधिकार प्राप्त है तथा इनकी प्राप्ति में जाति, भाषा, लिंग, धर्म आदि का भेदभाव नहीं हो सकता है।
3. सभी व्यक्ति को स्वाधीनता पूर्वक जीवन जीने एवं वैयक्तिक सुरक्षा का अधिकार प्राप्त है।
4. कानून की निगाह मे हर व्यक्ति बराबर है।

5. मानव अधिकारों का हनन करने वाले व्यक्ति के विरूद्ध कानूनी सहायता प्राप्त करने का हक है।

6. प्रत्येक व्यक्ति को अपने विचार व्यक्त करने की स्वतंत्रता है।

7. हर व्यक्ति को अपने देश की सीमा के भीतर कही भी आने जाने ओर बसने का अधिकार है।

8. किसी भी व्यक्ति को राष्ट्र की नागरिकता प्राप्ति का अधिकार है।

9. हर बालिग स्त्री पुरूष को बिना किसी जाति, राष्ट्रीयता, धर्म की रूकावटों के आपस में विवाह करने का अधिकार है।

10. किसी व्यक्ति को मनमाने ढंग से अपनी सम्पति से वंचित नहीं किया जा सकता है।

11. प्रत्येक व्यक्ति को अपने धर्म के अनुसार जीने का अधिकार है।

12. हर व्यक्ति को मत देने और अपने देश के मतदान में चुने जाने का अधिकार है।

13. हर व्यक्ति को अपने देश की सरकारी नौकरियों को प्राप्त करने का समान अधिकार है।

14. प्रत्येक व्यक्ति को समान कार्य के लिए बिना भेदभाव के समान मजदूरी पाने का अधिकार है।

15. प्रत्येक व्यक्ति को एक सामान्य जीवन स्तर, स्वास्थ्य, खाना, कपड़ा आदि को प्राप्त करने का हक है।

16. प्रत्येक व्यक्ति को शिक्षा प्राप्ति का हक है।

17. किसी को गुलामी या दासता की हालात में नहीं रखा जा सकता है।

संयुक्त राष्ट्र संघ द्वारा घोषित इन अधिकारों को मानव अधिकार कहा गया है जो संसार के समस्त प्राणियों के जन्मजात अधिकार है। संयुक्त राष्ट्र संघ के मानव अधिकारो से प्रेरणा प्राप्त कर संसार के अधिकांश स्वतंत्र राष्ट्रों ने इसे अपने अपने देश के संविधान में कानूनी रूप से मान्यता प्रदान की है।

1995 से 2004 तक के दशक को संयुक्त राष्ट्र संघ ने मानवाधिकर दशक घोषित किया था जिसके अन्तर्गत सारे संसार में यह प्रयास किया गया कि यह अधिकार सबको प्राप्त हो और समस्त मानव जाति को इन अधिकारों के बारे में जानकारी प्राप्त हो। ये मानव अधिकार मानव जाति के लिये अत्यंत आवश्यक है। ये उनके जन्मजात अधिकार है और मानव के व्यक्तित्व के विकास के लिये नितान्त आवश्यक है।

4 भारतीय संविधान में मौलिक अधिकार

संसार के प्रमुख लोकतंत्रों की तरह भारत के संविधान मे भी मौलिक अधिकारों को प्रस्तावित किया गया है। यह अधिकार हमारे जीवन के बुनियादी जरूरतों पर आधारित है। यह भारतीय संविधान की प्रस्तावना के उद्देश्यों, समानता, स्वतंत्रता और न्याय दिलाने की बात को कानूनी स्वरूप प्रदान करते है। यह भारतीय संविधान की महत्वपूर्ण विशेषता है और सभी नागरिकों के लिये आवश्यक है। यह मानवीय अधिकार ही है जिन्हें हमारे संविधान में मौलिक अधिकार का नाम दिया गया है।

भारतीय संविधान में छः मौलिक अधिकार प्रदान किये गये है–

1. स्वतंत्रता का अधिकार

2. समानता का अधिकार
3. शोषण के विरूद्व अधिकार
4. धार्मिक स्वतंत्रता का अधिकार
5. सांस्कृतिक और शैक्षिक अधिकार
6. संवैधानिक उपचार का अधिकार

(1) स्वतंत्रता का अधिकार –

इसका अर्थ है कि हमारे जीवन में किसी का दखल नहीं होना चाहिये न सरकार का न व्यक्ति का। इसके अन्तर्गत प्रत्येक नागरिक को कई तरह की स्वतंत्रताएं दी गयी है।

- अभिव्यक्ति की स्वतंत्रता
- शांतिपूर्ण ढंग से जमा होने की स्वतंत्रता
- संगठन एवं संघ बनाने की स्वतंत्रता
- देश में कहीं भी आने जाने की स्वतंत्रता
- देश के किसी भी भाग में रहने और बसने की स्वतंत्रता
- कोई भी काम धंधा करने, चुनने की स्वतंत्रता

संविधान के अनुसार किसी भी व्यक्ति को जीने के अधिकार और निजी स्वतंत्रता से वंचित नहीं किया जा सकता है। ये अधिकार कानूनी है, इसी के कारण सरकार या पुलिस को भी कुछ नियमों का पालन करना होता है जैसे बिना कारण बताये किसी को गिरफ्तार नहीं किया जा सकता है।

- गिरफ्तार या हिरासत में लिये गये व्यक्ति को सबसे निकट मजिस्ट्रेट के सामने 24 घंटे में प्रस्तुत करना जरूरी है।

- कानूनी मामलें में प्रत्येक व्यक्ति को वकील से विचार विमर्श या वकील रखने का अधिकार

(2) समानता का अधिकार –

सभी व्यक्ति कानून की नजरों में बराबर है कानून सब पर समान रूप से लागू होता है, इसीलिये इसे लोकतंत्र की बुनियाद कानूनी राज कहते है। प्रधानमंत्री हो या दूरदराज का खेतिहर मजदूर सभी पर एक ही तरह का कानून लागू होता है। समानता के अधिकार के कुछ उदाहरण जैसे सार्वजनिक स्थलों पर (दुकान, होटल, सिनेमाघर) किसी व्यक्ति को धर्म जाति सम्प्रदाय के आधार पर जाने से नहीं रोका जा सकता है। सरकारी नौकरियों पर भी यह सिद्धान्त लागू होता है। संवैधानिक प्रावधानों के अनुसार अनुसूचित जाति, जनजाति, पिछडी जातियों के लिये आरक्षण की व्यवस्था है।

(3) शोषण के खिलाफ अधिकार –

समानता के अधिकार मिलने के बाद यह जरूरी है कि नागरिकों का शोषण न हों। इस अधिकार के अन्तर्गत महिलाओं का शोषण किसी से बेगार या जबरन काम नहीं लिया जा सकता है। बाल मजदूरी का भी निषेध किया गया है। किसी कारखाने, रेलवे, बन्दरगाह के कम में 14 वर्ष से कम के बालको को नहीं लगाया जा सकता है।

(4) धार्मिक स्वतंत्रता का अधिकार –

भारत को धर्म निरपेक्ष राष्ट्र घोषित किया गया है। भारत में विविध धर्मों को मानने वाले लोग रहते है। कुछ ऐसे भी है जो किसी भी धर्म को नहीं मानते हैं भारत का कोई राजधर्म नहीं है। शासन सभी धर्मों को समान मानता है। इस मौलिक अधिकार के अन्तर्गत हर व्यक्ति को अपना धर्म मानने उसका आचरण करने

और प्रसार करने का अधिकार है। किसी व्यक्ति को जबरदस्ती धर्म परिवर्तन नहीं कराया जा सकता है। पशुबलि निषेध है। धार्मिक संस्थाओं में किसी धर्म विशेष का निर्देश नहीं दिया जा सकता है।

(5) सांस्कृतिक और शैक्षिक अधिकार –

इसके अन्तर्गत नागरिकों को अपनी किसी विशिष्ठ भाषा या संस्कृति को बचाने का अधिकार है। किसी भी सरकारी या अनुदान प्राप्त संस्था में धर्म या भाषा के आधार पर प्रवेश नहीं रोका जा सकता है। सभी अल्पसंख्यकों को अपनी पसन्द का शैक्षिक संस्थान स्थापित करने और चलाने का अधिकार है।

(6) संवैधानिक उपचार का अधिकार –

यह अधिकार मौलिक अधिकारों को गारन्टी प्रदान करने वाला अधिकार है। यह हमारे मौलिक अधिकारों को प्रभावी बनाता है। इसी के अन्तर्गत यदि हमारे किसी मौलिक अधिकार का हनन हो रहा हो तो हम अदालत जा सकते है और समस्या का निदान पा सकते है। डॉ. अम्बेडकर ने संवैधानिक उपचार के अधिकार को संविधान की आत्मा कहा था। इस अधिकार के अन्तर्गत सर्वोच्च न्यायालय या उच्च न्यायालय को मौलिक अधिकार के मामले में उसे लागू कराने के लिये निर्देश जारी कराने का अधिकार है, जिसे रिट कहते है। रिट के द्वारा कोई भी व्यक्ति मौलिक अधिकारों के उल्लंघन के लिये न्याय प्राप्त कर सकता है और अपराधी को दंडित किया जा सकता है।

आवश्यकतानुसार मौलिक अधिकारों का दायरा बढ़ाया भी जा सकता है। जैसे स्वास्थ्य, रक्षा के अधिकार, काम के अधिकार, जीने के जरूरी आवश्यकताओं के अधिकार आदि को मौलिक अधिकार में डालने की बात बराबर उठायी जा रही है। इस प्रकार

भारतीय संविधान के मौलिक अधिकार भारतीय नागरिकों को, जीने की सुरक्षा एंव अपने व्यक्तित्व के सर्वांगीण विकास के अवसर प्रदान करते है।

मानव अधिकार एवं मौलिक अधिकार की प्रस्तावना

1. मानव अधिकार अवधारणा एवं अधिकार पर परिचर्चा की जायेगी।
2. प्रमुख मानव अधिकारों के सम्बन्धित उदाहरण एवं व्याख्या का चार्ट प्रस्तुत कर उस पर चर्चा की जायेगी।
3. भारतीय संविधान में मौलिक अधिकार का चार्ट बताकर छात्राओं की सहायता से उसकी व्याख्या आयोजित की जायेगी।
4. मौलिक अधिकारों के सन्दर्भ में भावी शिक्षकों का योगदान विषय पर सामूहिक परिचर्चा आयोजित की जायेगी।

अध्ययन अध्यापन क्रियाएं –

1. मौलिक अधिकार विषय से सम्बन्धित समाचार पत्रों की सूचनाओं को विषय शिक्षण में किया जायेगा एवं उस पर चर्चा की जायेगी
2. मानव अधिकार दिवस 10 दिसम्बर के आयोजन की लघु नाटिका का प्रदर्शन किया जायेगा।
3. मानवाधिकारों की आवश्यकता एवं महत्व विषय पर कक्षा में समूह परिचर्चा की आयोजना की जायेगी।
4. भावी शिक्षक को विषयवस्तु से सम्बन्धित कहानी सुनाकर एवं उस पर परिचर्चा कर कार्य मूल्याकंन किया जायेगा।

मूल्याकंन प्रश्न –

1. 10 दिसम्बर को कौनसा अन्तर्राष्ट्रीय पर्व मनाया जाता है?

2. प्रमुख मानव अधिकार किन किन मूल्यों पर आधारित है?

3. संविधान में मौलिक अधिकारों को कानूनी मान्यता क्यों प्रदान की गयी है?

4. समानता के मौलिक अधिकार से सम्बन्धित कोई तीन उदाहरण दीजिये?

5. ईद के दिन रफीक मस्जिद में नमाज पढने जाता हैं यह उसका कौनसा मौलिक अधिकर है?

6. राधा और रमेश दोनो बांध पर मजदूरी करने गये। रमेश को 40 रूपये एवं राधा को 30 रूपये दिये गये इसमें कौनसे मौलिक अधिकार का हनन हुआ है?

7. विधायक के बेटे रमेश और मजदूर के बेटे सुरेश ने एक सरकारी बस में आग लगा दी। दोनों के दण्ड में अन्तर क्यों नहीं होना चाहिये? दोनों को एक साथ दण्ड दिया जाना किस मौलिक अधिकार के अन्तर्गत आता है?

8. मौलिक अधिकारों के अतिक्रमण की घटनाओं का समाज पर क्या प्रभाव पड़ता है? समाज में शांति और व्यवस्था बनी रहे इसके लिए मौलिक अधिकारों से सम्बन्धित कौन कौनसी क्रियाएं/उपाय अपनाये जाने चाहिये?

इकाई स – भारतीय संविधान में मौलिक दायित्व

Fundamental Duties according to constitution

उपइकाई –

1. मौलिक अधिकारों की पृष्ठभूमि एवं प्रथम पांच मौलिक दायित्व
2. मौलिक दायित्व छः से दस एवं उनकी उपयोगिता

विशिष्ठ उद्धेश्य –

ज्ञान – स्नातक अध्यापक इस पाठ के अध्यापन की समाप्ति के उपरान्त निम्नांकित तथ्यों का पुनःस्मरण एवं पुनः पहचान कर सकेंगे –

1. भारत के संविधान में 42 वें संशोधन के अन्तर्गत 1977 में संविधान में एक नये अनुच्छेद 51 ए संविधान के भाग चतुर्थ के अन्तर्गत मौलिक दायित्वों का समावेश किया गया।
2. भारतीय संविधान के अनुच्छेद 29 के अन्तर्गत जो मौलिक अधिकार नागरिकों को दिये गये है संविधान द्वारा प्रदत्त में मौलिक दायित्व उन्ही ने जुड़े हुए है।
3. संविधान में प्रदत मौलिक दायित्व भारतीय संविधान की प्रस्तावना में दिये गये मूल्यों पर आधारित है जिनमें नागरिकों से अपने देश के प्रति कुछ दायित्वों के निर्वाह की अपेक्षा की गयी हैं
4. छात्राध्यापक प्रमुख मौलिक दायित्वों का पुनःस्मरण कर सकेंगे। उदाहरण स्वरूप राष्ट्रीय ध्वज एवं राष्ट्रीय गान का सम्मान, अपने देश के सम्प्रभुता की रक्षा करना, आवश्यकतानुसार राष्ट्र की सेवा करना, सांस्कृतिक धरोहरों की रक्षा करना, अपने पर्यावरण की रक्षा करना आदि।

अवबोध –

1. छात्राध्यापक मौलिक दायित्वों को संविधान में शामित्व किये जाने के कारण बतायेंगे।

2. संविधान में प्रदत विविध मौलिक दायित्वों के उदाहरण प्रस्तुत करेंगे।

3. छात्र मौलिक दायित्वों का संविधान में दी गयी प्रस्तावना के मूल्यों से सम्बन्ध स्थापित करेंगे।

4. संविधान में प्रदत मौलिक आधिकारों एवं मौलिक दायित्वों मे अन्तर कर सकेंगे।

कौशल –

छात्राध्यापक मौलिक दायित्वों से सम्बन्धित चार्ट बना सकेंगे।

ज्ञानोपयोग – किसी नयी परिस्थिति या वातावरण के प्रस्तुत किये जाने पर अपने मौलिक दायित्वों से सम्बन्धित निर्णय ले सकेंगे।

पाठ्यवस्तु विश्लेषण –

ऐतिहासिक पृष्ठभूमि –

26 जनवरी, 1950 को लागू किये गये भारतीय संविधान में मौलिक कर्त्तव्यों का उल्लेख नहीं था। 1977 में संविधान के 42 वें संशोधन के अर्न्तगत एक नये अनुच्छेद द्वारा संविधान के चौथे भाग में 51 ए जोड़कर मौलिक दायित्वों को संविधान का भाग बनाया गया। भारतीय संविधान की प्रस्तावना ने जिन मूल्यों की घोषणा की गयी है उनकी पूर्ति के लिये नागरिको से ये अपेक्षा की जाती है कि वे राष्ट्र के प्रति कुछ मौलिक कर्तव्यों की पालना करे। संविधान के ये मौलिक कर्तव्य उन्हीं मूल्यों के अनुरूप है।

भारतीय संविधान में प्रस्तावित मौलिक कर्तव्य इस प्रकार से है –

भारत के प्रत्येक नागरिक का कर्तव्य होगा कि वह –

1. संविधान का पालन करे और उसके आदर्शों, संस्थाओं, राष्ट्रध्वज और राष्ट्रगान का आदर करे।
2. स्वतंत्रता के लिए हमारे राष्ट्रीय आन्दोलन को प्रेरित करने वाले उच्च आदर्शों को ह्रदय में संजोए व उनका पालन करे।
3. भारत की प्रभुता, एकता व अखण्डता की रक्षा करे व उसे अक्षुण रखे।
4. देश की रक्षा करे व आव्हान किए जाने पर राष्ट्र की सेवा करे।
5. भारत के सभी लोगो में समरसता व समानता भातृत्व की भावना का निर्माण करे जो धर्म, भाषा, प्रदेश या वर्ण पर आधारित सभी भेदभावों से परे हो, ऐसी प्रथाओं को त्यागे जो स्त्रियों के सम्मान के विरूद्ध है।
6. हमारी सामाजिक संस्कृति की गौरवशाली परम्परा का महत्व समझे और उसका परिरक्षण करें।
7. प्राकृतिक पर्यावरण की जिसके अन्तर्गत वन, झील, नदी और वन्यजीव है, की रक्षा करे और उसका संवर्द्धन करे तथा प्राणी मात्र के प्रति दया भाव रखे।
8. वैज्ञानिक दृष्टिकोण, मानववाद और ज्ञानार्जन के साथ सुधार की भावना का विकास करे।
9. सार्वजनिक सम्पति को सुरक्षित रखे और हिंसा से दूर रहें।

10. व्यक्तिगत और सामुहिक गतिविधियों के सभी क्षेत्रों में उत्कर्ष की और बढ़ने का सतत प्रयास करे जिससे राष्ट्र निरन्तर बढ़ते हुए प्रयत्न और उपलब्धि की नई ऊंचाईयों को छू ले।

संविधान में दिये गये इन मौलिक कर्तव्यों की अनुपालना हमारे भावी नागरिक मन से करे इस हेतु यह आवश्यक है कि इन मौलिक दायित्वों का व्यापक रूप से प्रचार और प्रसार किया जाये तथा भावी नागरिकों के मन में यह आस्था उत्पन्न की जाये कि इनके पालन द्वारा व्यक्ति के स्वयं के जीवन में, समाज और राष्ट्र के जीवन में स्वतंत्रता समानता बंधुत्व जैसे मुल्यों का जागरण किया जा सकता है और इसके द्वारा समाज के शौषण और हिंसा से मुक्त कर वहां शांति एवं सद्भाव का पर्यावरण निर्मित किया जा सकता है।

अध्ययन अध्यापन क्रियाएं – प्रस्तावना सम्बन्धित शैक्षणिक क्रिया –

छात्राध्यापकों को दो समूहों में विभक्त कर एक समूह द्वारा पांच पांच उन अधिकारों की सूची बनाने को कहा जायेगा जो उन्हें परिवार एवं स्कूल में प्राप्त होने चाहिये। अधिकारों की सूची बन जाने पर उन्हें दूसरे समूह को वितरित कर उनसे सम्बन्धित परिवार एवं विद्यालय में उनके द्वारा किये जाने वाले पांच पांच सम्बन्धित दायित्वों की सूची बनाने को कहा जायेगा। बाद में उन अधिकारों एवं कर्तव्यों को चॉक बोर्ड पर लिखकर उन्हें पढ़वाकर कुछ प्रश्न पूछकर एक परिचर्चा आयोजित की जायेगी।

1. संविधान में वर्णित मौलिक अधिकारों के चार्ट की प्रस्तुती की जायेगी।
2. संविधान में वर्णित मौलिक दायित्वों के चार्ट की प्रस्तुती कर परिचर्चा की जायेगी।

3. समाचार पत्रों में प्रकाशित नागरिकों द्वारा अपने किसी दायित्व की अनुपालना सम्बन्धित विशेष समाचारों का वाचन कर उस पर परीचर्चा की जायेगी।

4. मौलिक दायित्वों से सम्बन्धित प्रमुख महापुरूषों विद्वानों के कथन एवं उनसे सम्बन्धित प्रश्न पूछकर उनकी व्याख्या की जायेगी।

5. मौलिक दायित्वों की अनुपालना से सम्बन्धित कहानी सुनाकर उस पर चर्चा की जायेगी।

6. कविताओं का वाचन एवं उसका पाठ कर तथा उस पर परिचर्चा की जायेगी।

7. मौलिक दायित्वों से सम्बन्धित संगोष्ठी वाद विवाद प्रतियोगिता आदि का आयोजना की जायेगी।

मूल्याकंन –

1. भारतीय संविधान में किन किन मौलिक आधिकारों का समावेश किया गया है?

2. मौलिक अधिकारों ओर मौलिक कर्तव्य एक दूसरे के पूरक क्यों है?

3. भारतीय संविधान में मौलिक दायित्वों का समन्वय कब किया गया?

4. राष्ट्रीय ध्वज एवं राष्ट्र गान का सम्मान हमे किस प्रकार करना चाहिये? इसके कुछ उदाहरण दीजिये?

5. प्राकृतिक पर्यावरण अन्तर्गत किन किन वस्तुओं को सम्मिलित किया जाता है?

6. अपने प्राकृतिक पर्यावरण की सुरक्षा हम किस प्रकार कर सकते है?

7. सार्वजनिक सम्पति कितने प्रकार की होती है?
8. सार्वजनिक सम्पति की सुरक्षा क्यों आवश्यक है?
9. विदेशी आक्रमण के समय नागरिकों के क्या दायित्व होते है?
10. विदेशी आक्रमण के समय देश की संप्रभुता और एकता की रक्षा नागरिक किन किन रूपों में कर सकते है?
11. नागरिक कर्तव्यों की अनुपालना का हमारे व्यक्तिगत ओर सामाजिक जीवन पर क्या प्रभाव पड़ता है?

इकाई द – संयुक्त राष्ट्र संघ द्वारा घोषित बाल अधिकार

Child Rights Declared by U.N.O.

उपइकाई –

1. बाल अधिकार (पृष्ठभूमि, आवश्यकता, महत्व, संप्रत्यय)
2. संयुक्त राष्ट्रसंघ द्वारा घोषित प्रमुख बाल अधिकार

विशिष्ठ उद्धेश्य –

भावी छात्राध्यापक इस पाठ की समाप्ति पर निम्नांकित तथ्यों का पुनःस्मरण करेंगे।

ज्ञान –

1. मानव अधिकरों का सम्प्रत्यय परिभाषा का पुनःस्मरण करेंगे।
2. संयुक्त राष्ट्र संघ द्वारा घोषित प्रमुख बाल अधिकारों का पुनःस्मरण करेंगे।

अवबोध –

1. मानव अधिकारों एवं बाल अधिकारों के मध्य अन्तर

करेंगे।

2. संयुक्त राष्ट्र संघ द्वारा बाल अधिकारों की उद्घोषणा के कारण बतायेंगे।
3. बाल अधिकर एवं छात्रों के व्यक्तित्व के सर्वांगीण विकास के बीच सम्बन्ध स्थापित करेंगे।

कौशल –

प्रमुख बाल अधिकारों को चार्ट में पढ़कर उनका वर्गीकरण करेंगे।

ज्ञानोपयोग –

कतिपय बाल अधिकारों के उल्लंघन की घटनाओं पर अपनी प्रतिक्रिया व्यक्त करेंगे।

पाठ्यवस्तु विश्लेषण –

पृष्ठभूमि –

संयुक्त राष्ट्र संघ द्वारा घोषित मानवअधिकारों से प्रेरणा लेकर संयुक्त राष्ट्र संघ की साधारण सभा ने 20 नवम्बर, 1959 को बाल अधिकारों की घोषणा की।

आवश्यकता –

चुंकि बालक को अपनी शारीरिक एवं मानसिक अपरिपक्वता के कारण जन्म के पूर्व एवं पश्चात् यथोचित कानूनी संरक्षण सहित विशेष संरक्षण एवं देखभाल की आवश्यकता है। इस आवश्यकता की पूर्ति बाल अधिकार द्वारा की जा सकती है।

सम्प्रत्यय –

संयुक्त राष्ट्र संघ के उद्धेश्यों के अनुसार मानव जाति अपना

सर्वोत्तम बालक को प्रदान करने हेतु प्रतिबद्ध है। इसलिये बाल अधिकारों का विशेष महत्व है।

बाल अधिकारों से तात्पर्य उन अवसरों एवं अधिकारों की घोषणा से है जिसके बालक अपना सर्वांगीण विकास कर सके और अभिभावकों, शैक्षिक संगठनों स्थानीय निकायों एवं राष्ट्रीय सरकारों द्वारा इन अधिकारों को प्राप्त कर सके। इन अधिकारों के उल्लंघन होने पर इनसे सम्बन्धित न्याय की प्राप्ति कर सके। इन अधिकारों की प्राप्ति स्वतंत्रता, समानता, सामाजिक न्याय प्राप्ति पर आधारित है।

सयुक्त राष्ट्र संघ के घोषणा पत्र में बाल अधिकार से सबंधित दस अनुच्छेद है। इन अनुच्छेदों के अन्तर्गत निम्नलिखित प्रमुख बाल अधिकारों की प्रस्तुती की गयी है –

1. बालक के व्यक्तित्व के शारीरिक मानसिक नैतिक आध्यात्मिक और सामाजिक विकास हेतु उसे अनुकूल अवसर एवं सुविधाएं प्रदान करना।
2. प्रत्येक बच्चे को जन्म से ही अपना नाम व राष्ट्रीयता अपनाने का अधिकार हो।
3. बालक को परिवार में उसके माता पिता द्वारा उसके संरक्षण विशेषकर स्वास्थ्य की देखभाल की व्यवस्था करनी होगी। उन्हें आवश्यकतानुसार विशेष चिकित्सा सुविधा एवं शिक्षा दी जावेगी।
4. बालक को उसके माता पिता का भरपूर स्नेह मिलेगा तथा उनसे बालक को विलग नहीं किया जायेगा।
5. प्रत्येक बालक को कम से कम प्राथमिक स्तर तक निःशुल्क एवं अनिवार्य शिक्षा प्राप्त होगी। इस शिक्षा का प्रमुख उद्धेश्य उसे समाज का उपयोगी नागरिक

बनाना होगा।

6. बच्चे की शिक्षा उसके लिये खेल एवं मनोरंजन की जिम्मेदारी का प्रमुख दायित्व माता पिता एवं सामाजिक एवं प्रशासनिक अधिकारियों का होगा।

7. बच्चे को सभी प्रकार की उपेक्षा निर्दयता, शोषण, के विरूद्ध संरक्षण मिलेगा एवं किसी भी रूप में उसका शोषण नहीं होगा।

8. एक न्यूनतम आयु के पूर्व बालक को किसी रोजगार में नहीं रखा जायेगा तथा किसी ऐसे कार्य में नहीं लगाया जायेगा जिसके उसके स्वास्थ्य एवं शिक्षा में बाधा पड़े।

9. बालक को समानता का हक मिलेगा। उसका पालन पोषण, समझदारी सहिष्णुता मैत्री भाव, शांति एवं विश्वबंधुतव की भावना से किया जायेगा।

10. संयुक्त राष्ट्र संघ के सदस्यों की सरकारें बाल अधिकारों के व्यापक प्रचार प्रसार का कार्य करेंगी।

प्रस्तावना सम्बन्धी क्रिया (Introductry Activity) –

संयुक्त राष्ट्र संघ U. N. O. द्वारा घोषित मानव अधिकारों का चार्ट प्रस्तुत कर उससे सम्बन्धित प्रश्न पूछकर की जायेगी।

अध्ययन अध्यापन क्रियाएं –

1. मानव अधिकारों के सम्बन्धित चार्ट की प्रस्तुती कर उस पर परिचर्चा की जायेगी।

2. समाचार पत्रों में प्रकाशित बाल अधिकारों के उल्लंघन

एवं शोषण की घटनाओं को प्रस्तुत कर उन पर परिचर्चा आयोजित की जायेगी।

3. विद्यालय में विद्यार्थियों को किन किन अधिकारों की प्राप्ति होनी चाहिये इससे सम्बन्धित उनके सुझावों को आमंत्रित कर प्रस्ताव तैयार किया जायेगा।

मूल्याकंन –

1. संयुक्त राष्ट्र संघ द्वारा बाल अधिकारों की उद्‌घोषणा कब की गयी?
2. बाल अधिकारों की उद्‌घोषणा के पीछे प्रमुख कारण कौन कौन से थे?
3. बाल अधिकारों की परिभाषा अपनी शब्दावली में प्रस्तुत कीजिये।
4. मानव अधिकारों एवं बाल अधिकारों में क्या समानता पायी जाती है?
5. बाल अधिकारों और मानव अधिकारों के बीच प्रमुख अन्तर क्या है?
6. परिवार द्वारा प्रदान किये जाने वाले बाल अधिकारों के कुछ उदाहरण दीजिये।
7. विद्यालय में आपकी कक्षा में आपको कौन कौनसे अधिकार मिलने चाहिये?
8. विद्यालय द्वारा समाजसेवा शिविर मे जाने से रोक दिये जाने पर आप इस सम्बन्ध में क्या कार्यवाही करेंगे।
9. आपके कक्षाध्यापक द्वारा आपके साथी को शारीरिक यातना दिये जाने पर ऐसी घटनाओं की पुनरावृति

रोकने के लिये आप अपने सहपाठियों के साथ मिलकर क्या कार्यवाहीं करेंगे।

इकाई य – शांति शिक्षा के भावी सक्रियतावादी अध्यापक का व्यवहारगत स्वरूप

The Behavioural Pattern of Prospective Teachers and its Implementation for Peace Education

उपइकाई –

1. भावी अध्यापक
2. शांति शिक्षा के अध्यापक
3. शांति शिक्षा के सक्रियतावादी अध्यापक का व्यवहारगत स्वरूप
4. शांति शिक्षा के भावी सक्रियतावादी अध्यापक की भूमिका

विशिष्ट उद्देश्य–

ज्ञान – स्नातक अध्यापक इस पाठ को पढ़ने के उपरान्त निम्नांकित तथ्यों का प्रत्यास्मरण एवं पुर्न पहचान कर सकेंगे।

1. भावी अध्यापकों के व्यक्तित्व एवं दायित्व का स्मरण एवं पुर्नपहचान कर सकेंगे।
2. शांति शिक्षा के सक्रियतावादी अध्यापक के रूप में अपनी भूमिका को समझ सकेंगे।

अवबोध –

1. सामान्य अध्यापक एवं सक्रियतावादी अध्यापक में अन्तर करेंगे।
2. एक अध्यापक को शांति शिक्षा हेतु सक्रियतावादी

अध्यापक होना क्यों आवश्यक है इसके कारण बतायेंगे।

3. शांति शिक्षा के सक्रियतावादी अध्यापक के पाठ्यक्रमिक एवं पाठ्यसहगामी क्रियाओं के क्षेत्र में की जाने वाली शैक्षिक क्रियाओं के उदाहरण देंगे।

कौशल–

1. सामूहिक परिचर्चा के सदस्य के रूप में विचार अभिव्यक्ति का कौशल उत्पन्न होगा।
2. इकाई से संबंधित चार्ट को देखकर परिचर्चा में भाग लेंगे।

अभिवृति –

शांति शिक्षा के प्रशिक्षण के उपरान्त शांति शिक्षा के सक्रियतावादी अध्यापक बनने की प्रेरणा जागृत होगी।

1. भावी शिक्षक (Prospective Teachers)–

भावी अध्यापक कल के भारत के भविष्य के निर्माणकर्ता है। आज जैसा उनका प्रशिक्षण होगा वेसा वे कल का भारत बनायेंगे। कोठारी कमीशन ने सत्य ही कहा है कि भारत के भविष्य का निर्माण उसकी कक्षाओं में हो रहा है। भारत के भावी नागरिक जो हमारी कक्षाओं मे बैठे है उन्हे हम जिस रूप में तैयार करेंगे वैसा ही कल का भारत बनेगा। भारत संसार का सबसे बडा लोकतांत्रिक गणराज्य है। इसने अपनी स्वतंत्रता, महात्मा गांधी के नेतृत्व में स्वतंत्रता, समानता और बन्धुत्व, सामाजिक न्याय, विश्व बन्धुत्व आदि मूल्यों को लेकर प्राप्त की है। गांधी जी का सारा जीवन अहिंसा पर आधारित था और हमारा स्वतंत्रता संग्राम भी अहिंसात्मक है। यह विश्व इतिहास का अकेला उदाहरण है जहां 200 वर्षो के विदेशी आन्दोलन को सत्याग्रह द्वारा आन्दोलन

चलाकर शांतिपूर्ण अहिंसात्मक रूप से स्वतंत्रता की प्राप्ति की गयी। आज की भारतीय शिक्षा का प्रमुख उद्धेश्य प्रभावी लोकतांत्रिक नागरिकों का निर्माण करना है यह जिम्मेदारी भावी शिक्षकों पर है कि वे लोकतंत्रिक गुणों से परिपूर्ण नागरिक तैयार करे। लोकतंत्र के प्रभावी नागरिकों से तात्पर्य ऐसे नागरिकों से है जिनका व्यक्तित्व सत्य, अहिंसा, स्नेह, सद्भाव, धर्मनिरपेक्षता, समानता, स्वतंत्रता बन्धुत्व जैसे मूल्यों पर आधारित है इन नागरिकों का निमार्ण आपको भावी अध्यापकों को करना है। इस दृष्टि से भावी अध्यापकों का प्रशिक्षण अत्यन्त महत्वपूर्ण है।

2. शांति शिक्षा के अध्यापक –

शिक्षक संस्कृति का परिमार्जन परिशोधन एवं हस्तान्तरण कर महत्वपूर्ण उत्तरदायित्व निभाता है और साथ ही शिक्षण, अनुसंधान एवं प्रसार का कार्य भी करता है। शांति शिक्षक वे शिक्षक है जो शांति की भावना का अपने विद्यार्थियों एवं वातावरण में सृजन कर सके और विद्यार्थियों को परस्पर प्रेम सहयोग सद्भावना के साथ नैतिक चेतना का विकास करते हुए शांतिपूर्ण विश्व के निर्माण हेतु शैक्षिक प्रक्रिया को कुशलतापूर्वक चला सके एवं भावी विश्व में वसुधैव कुटुम्बकम की भावना को स्थापित करते हुए आनन्दमयी विश्व का निर्माण कर सके।

शान्ति शिक्षक विद्यार्थियों को विद्यालय एवं समाज में सकारात्मक विचारों के साथ दूसरों के विचारो को आदर सहित स्वीकार करना एवं मानव गरिमा को सम्मान तथा दूसरों के साथ व्यवहार में ऐसी सोच विकसित करना सीखता है जो स्वयं के लिये चाहता है। शांति शिक्षक संघर्ष के मूल कारणों की समझ विकसित कर उसे सुलझाने की समझ को भी विकसित करता है। शांति शिक्षक छात्रों को श्रेष्ठ इंसान बनाने तथा समाज एवं राष्ट्रीय हित के साथ मानवता के विकास के लिये तैयार करता है। शांति शिक्षक

विद्यार्थियों को जीवन मूल्यों के प्रति जागरूक कर छोटे व बड़ों के साथ उचित व्यवहार करना सिखाते हुए शांतिपूर्ण मन स्थिति का निर्माण करने की कला सीखाता है। शान्ति शिक्षक स्वयं अपने अवगुणों के प्रति भी सचेत रहता है, जिससे इसके दुष्प्रभाव विद्यार्थियों पर नहीं आये।

शांति शिक्षक शांति विषय पर संवाद, परिचर्चा, योजना बनाने में विद्यार्थियों की सहायता करता है तथा विविध त्यौहार एवं पर्वों के माध्यम से विद्यालय में विविध राष्ट्रीय दिवसों के माध्यम से छात्रों को पूर्ण सहयोग एवं सहभागिता सुनिश्चित कराते हुए प्रेम एवं सद्भावना विकसित करता है। छात्रों को दूसरों की भावनाओ एवं संवेदनाओं को समझने के साथ श्रेष्ठ व्यवहार हेतु प्रेरित करता है। शांति शिक्षक विद्यार्थियों की आर्थिक सामाजिक परिस्थिति से परिचित होकर सहानुभूतिपूर्वक व्यवहार कर विद्यार्थियों के सर्वांगीण विकास को दृष्टिगत रखते हुए शांति शिक्षा को बढ़ाने में सहायता देता है।

3. शांति शिक्षा के भावी सक्रियतावादी अध्यापक का व्यवहारगत स्वरूप –

अध्यापक के लिए सक्रियतावादी होना जरूरी है। अध्यापक का कार्य अपने विद्यार्थियों के व्यवहार का परिमार्जन और परिवर्तन करना है। सरल शब्दों में अपने विद्यार्थियों को व्यावहारिक रूप में जनतंत्र का प्रभावी नागरिक बनाना है। व्यवहार परिवर्तन के अभिकर्ता के रूप में अध्यापक का स्वयं का व्यवहार भी जनतांत्रिक मूल्यों पर आधारित होना चाहियै। उसके व्यक्तित्व की व्यावहारिक क्रियाएं जनतांत्रिक मूल्यों पर आधारित होनी चाहिये। उदाहरणस्वरूप अध्यापक को विद्यार्थियों के साथ अपने सम्बन्ध में स्वतंत्रता, समानता एवं बंधुत्व के मूल्यों की झलक मिलनी चाहिये।

अध्यापक के विद्यालयी जीवन में उसके व्यवहार में निम्नाकिंत मूल्यों को स्थान मिलना चाहिये –

1. वह अपने विद्यार्थियों के साथ समानता का व्यवहार करे। उसकी नजरों में समस्त विद्यार्थी समान होने चाहिये। उसे अपने विद्यार्थियों के साथ धर्म, जाति, लिंग के आधार पर प्रतिभाशाली पिछड़े हुए आदि के आधार पर भेद नहीं करना चाहिये।

2. उसे अपने विद्यार्थियों को कक्षा के अन्तर्गत अथवा विद्यालय में अभिव्यक्ति की स्वतंत्रता देनी चाहिये उन्हें विद्यालय में शान्तिपूर्ण रूप से अपनी समस्याओं को रखने का अवसर मिलना चाहिये।

3. उन्हें विद्यालय में अपने शैक्षिक एवं सांस्कृतिक अध्ययन के लिये विविध संगठन, क्लब आदि बनाने की स्वतंत्रता होनी चाहिये।

4. उन्हे अपनी रूचि एवं क्षमता अनुसार विषय एवं संकाय चयन का अधिकार होना चाहिए।

5. उन्हे अकारण अनुचित एवं विशेषकर शारीरिक दण्ड बिल्कुल नहीं दिया जाना चाहिये।

6. शैक्षणिक संस्थाओं में विद्यार्थियों का शोषण जाति या लिंग पर आधारित नहीं होना चाहिये। उनसे किसी भी प्रकार का बेगार नहीं लिया जाना चाहिए।

7. विद्यार्थियों को शिक्षण संस्थाओं में किसी धर्म विशेष की प्रार्थना एवं अन्य क्रियाओं के लिये बाध्य नहीं किया जाना चाहिये।

8. विद्यालयों में समस्त धार्मिक उत्सवों का आयोजन सामुहिक रूप से किया जाना चाहिये।

9. विद्यालय में होने वाले विद्यालयी संसद एवं अन्य संस्थाओं के चुनाव में मत देने और खडे होने का अधिकार होना चाहिए।
10. बालक को परिवार एवं विद्यालय में उनके स्वास्थ्य के देखभाल की पर्याप्त व्यवस्था होनी चाहिये।
11. विद्यालय में उसके लिये खेलकूद एवं मनोरंजन का समुचित वातावरण एवं अवसर मिलने चाहिये।

अन्त में लिखा जा सकता है कि बालक को अपने अध्यापकों एवं अभिभावकों का स्नेहपूर्ण मार्गदर्शन मिलना चाहिये।

4. शांति शिक्षा के सक्रियता वादी भावी अध्यापक की भूमिका –

उपरोक्त जीवन दर्शन एवं व्यवहार का अपनाने वाले अध्यापक सहज एवं स्वाभाविक रूप से शांति शिक्षण का कार्य प्रभावी ढ़ंग से कर सकते है। इस प्रकार का जीवन जीने वाले और अपने विद्यार्थियों में ऐसा ही व्यवहार परिवर्तन लाने के लिए निरन्तर संघर्षशील अध्यापक को हम शांति शिक्षा के सक्रियतावादी अध्यापक कहकर सम्बोधित कर सकते है।

अतः भावी अध्यापक को शिक्षा के इस प्रमुख उद्धेश्य एवं क्रिया शांति की शिक्षा के लिए निरन्तर संघर्षशील रहना है तथा उसे शांति शिक्षा का सक्रियतावादी अध्यापक बनना है। इस कार्य को उसे अपने विद्यालय परिसर में विद्यार्थियों के साथ अपने सम्बन्धों में तथ अपने कक्षा कक्ष क्रियाओं में समाहित करना होगा। उसे अपने विषय एवं पाठ्यवस्तु को पढ़ाते समय पढ़ायी जाने वाली इकाई से सम्बन्धित मूल्यों के लिए अपने छात्रों को अभिप्रेरित करने एवं उन मूल्यों को अपने जीवन में व्यावहारिक रूप से उतारने का प्रशिक्षण देना होगा। यह तब सम्भव होगा जब अध्यापक अपनी

पाठ्यपुस्तक पर अधिकार रखते हुए पूर्व तैयारी के साथ इन मूल्यों के जागरण का कार्य कविता, कहानी, संस्मरण, नाटक, उदाहरण समूह चर्चा आदि विभिन्न क्रियाओं को आयोजन करते हुए करेगा।

शांति शिक्षा अधिक प्रभावपूर्ण तरीके से विद्यालय के विविध पाठ्यसहगामी क्रियाओं की आयोजना द्वारा दी जा सकती है। क्यों कि बालक के व्यक्तित्व के भावनात्मक पक्षों को (विभिन्न संवेदनाओं और मूल्यों को) विविध पाठ्यसहगामी क्रियाओं की आयोजना और उनकी सक्रिय भागीदारी द्वारा किया जा सकता है।

विद्यालय संसद की आयोजना, विविध शैक्षणिक पर्यटनों की आयोजना विद्यालय में विविध राष्ट्रीय एवं अन्तर्राष्ट्रीय एवं विविध धार्मिक पर्वों का उल्लासमय आयोजनएवं विविध प्रकार की सामूहिक सेवा से सम्बन्धित प्रोजेक्ट कार्य इस दिशा में प्रभावी रूप से कार्य कर सकते है।

इस प्रकार शांति शिक्षा का सक्रियतावादी अध्यापक वो है जो हर क्षण सावधानी पूर्वक इन मूल्यों की स्थापना की विविध क्रियाओं में भागीदार रहता है।

अध्ययन अध्यापन क्रियाएं – प्रस्तावना सम्बधी शैक्षणिक क्रियाऐं

1. शांति शिक्षा के शिक्षक के रूप में अध्यापक के व्यक्तित्व एवं दायित्व संबंधित परिचर्चा की आयोजना की जायेगी।
2. शांति शिक्षा से संबंधित विद्यालय में आयोजित किये जाने वाले विभिन्न उत्सवों के आयोजन की प्रायोजना की रूपरेखा का निर्माण किया जायेगा।
3. शांति शिक्षा से संबंधित विभिन्न शैक्षणिक क्रिया कलापों से संबंधित चार्ट तैयार करवाया जायेगा।

4. शांति शिक्षा से संबंधित सृजनात्मक कार्य जैसे कोई गीत पोस्टर, कहानी, सुभाषित (आर्दश वाक्य) नारा आदि तैयार करवाया जायेगा।

मूल्यांकन प्रश्न –

1. भारतीय संविधान की प्रस्तावना में किन – किन प्रमुख मूल्यों का उल्लेख हुआ है।
2. भारतीय संविधान की प्रस्तावना के मूल्यों का शांति शिक्षा के अध्यापक के लिये क्या महत्व है।
3. एक सामान्य शिक्षक एवं शांति शिक्षा के सक्रियतावादी शिक्षक के बीच अन्तर कीजिये।
4. शांति शिक्षा के लिये विद्यालय में किन – किन उत्सवों की विशेष आयोजना की जानी चाहिये।
5. शांति शिक्षा के शिक्षक के रूप में कक्षाकक्ष के अंतर्गत अध्यापक द्वारा किये जाने वाले किन्हीं चार व्यवहारों के उदाहरण दीजीये।
6. शांति शिक्षा के प्रशिक्षण के कार्यक्रम का आपके व्यक्तित्व विकास में क्या योगदान है।

इकाई र – शांति शिक्षा एवं निःशस्त्रीकरण

Peace Education and Disarmament

1. आवश्यकता एवं महत्व
2. निःशस्त्रीकरण का अर्थ
3. निःशस्त्रीकरण एवं उस हेतु किये गये प्रयत्न
4. U.N.O. के निःशस्त्रीकरण हेतु किये गये प्रयास

5 निःशस्त्रीकरण के प्रयास एवं अध्यापक की भूमिका

विशिष्ट उद्देश्य

ज्ञान – इस पाठ की समाप्ति पर भावी अध्यापक निम्नांकित तथ्यों का पुनःस्मरण कर सकेगें।

1. शांति की प्राप्ति में शस्त्रीकरण एक बहुत बड़ी बाधा है
2. लीग ऑफ नेशन्स और संयुक्त राष्ट्र की असफलता का प्रमुख कारण भी राष्ट्रों के बीच शस्त्रीकरण की होड है।
3. हिंसात्मक उपकरणों का रखाव पारिवारिक एवं सामाजिक शांति की बहुत बड़ी बाधा है।
4. निःशस्त्रीकरण पर चर्चा एवं उसके लिए प्रयत्नशील रहना आज की सबसे बड़ी आवश्यकता है।

अवबोध –

1. छात्रा शस्त्रीकरण के कारण बतायेगी।
2. छात्रा शस्त्रीकरण का पारिवारिक एवं सामाजिक एवं सामाजिक शांति और सद्भाव से संबंध बैठा सकेंगी।
3. छात्रा निःशस्त्रीकरण की दिशा में न्छव्‌ द्वारा किये किये जाने वाले प्रयासों के उदाहरण देंगी।

कौशल –

1. शांति शिक्षा एवं निःशस्त्रीकरण पर समूह चर्चा कर प्रभावी मौखिक अभिव्यक्ति की कुशलता प्राप्त करेंगे।
2. विषय से संबधित चार्ट एवं मानचित्र पढ़ने एवं उसकी व्याख्या में कुशल हो सकेंगें।

ज्ञानोपयोग –

इस विषय पर लघु संसद में परिचर्चा करेंगें एवं प्रस्ताव पारित कर सकेंगे।

पाठ्यवस्तु विश्लेषण

शांति शिक्षा एवं निःशस्त्रीकरण

Peace Education and Disarmament

1. आवश्यकता एवं महत्व : –

शस्त्रीकरण शांति स्थापना की बड़ी बाधा है। शांति शिक्षा से निःशस्त्रीकरण का गहरा सम्बन्ध है। आज हिंसा बढानें एवं मानसिक शांति एवं संतुलन को नष्ट करने में शस्त्रीकरण बहुत हद तक जिम्मेदार है। यह विशेषकर दो विश्व–युद्धों का भी प्रमुख कारण रहा है। लीग ऑफ नेशन्स की विफलता एवं संयुक्त राष्ट्र संघ के उद्देश्यों की पूर्ति में भी शस्त्रीकरण बहुत बड़ी बाधा बनकर उपस्थित हुआ है। युद्व का अन्त विश्व शांति की प्रमुख शर्त है और युद्व का अन्त बिना निःशस्त्रीकरण के संभव नहीं है। इतना ही नहीं स्थानीय पारिवारिक एवं राष्ट्रीय जीवन की शांति के मार्ग में शस्त्रीकरण आज एक बाधा बना हुआ है। परिवार में, विद्यालय में जो आये दिन हिंसा एव हत्या की घटनाऐं देखने सुनने को मिलती है उसका कारण भी शस्त्रों का प्रयोग ही है। भले ही वे छोटे रूप में रिवाल्वर या बंदूकों के गैरकानूनी प्रयोग के रूप में ही क्यों न हों। अतः यदि हम शांति की स्थापना शांति शिक्षा के माध्यम से करना चाहते है तो हमें आगे आने वाली पीढ़ी के मन में हिंसात्मक शस्त्रों के प्रति नफरत का भाव एवं उनकी समाप्ति की मुहिम छेड़ने का व्रत लेना ही होगा। पारिवारिक, समूह एवं राष्ट्रों के मध्य संघर्ष (conflicts) एक स्वाभाविक प्रक्रिया है अतः उनके अंत के प्रस्ताव, संघर्ष का शांतिपूर्ण हल पर हमें अमल करना ही

होगा और इस दिशा में निःशस्त्रीकरण की आवश्यकता एवं उसकी प्राप्ति के उपायों पर विशद् चर्चा करनी ही होगी।

2. निःशस्त्रीकरण का अर्थ :

निःशस्त्रीकरण से तात्पर्य उन हिंसात्मक उपकरणों को जिनमें विशेष रूप से छोटे उपकरण, बारूदी सुरंगे, व्यापक नर संहार के उपकरण शामिल है उनके प्रयोग पर रोक लगाना एवं धीरे धीरे उनकी समाप्ति के प्रयास करना है।

3. निःशस्त्रीकरण एवं उस हेतु किये गये प्रयत्न :

The United Nations Institute For Disarmament (UNDIR) में कहा गया है कि छोटे शस्त्र एवं बारूदी सुरंगे मानव सुरक्षा के मार्ग की बड़ी चुनौतियाँ है। हमें मालूम है कि जब कभी संघर्ष का अन्त हुआ है उसके बाद भी हिंसात्मक उपकरणों का अन्त नही हुआ है। उनका जखीरा या तो एकत्रित हो रहा है अथवा उसका गुप्त वितरण हुआ है। इनका प्रयोग पुनः अनेक अवसरों पर मानव को शारीरिक चोट पहुँचाने में किया गया है। हिंसात्मक उपकरणों के घातक शिकार सदैव निर्दोष नागरिक एंव विशेषकर बच्चे हुए है।

UNDIR का यही प्रयत्न रहा है है कि उन लोगों को प्रोत्साहित किया जाये (व्यक्तिगत समूह अथवा NGO संस्था रूप) जो हिंसक उपकरणों के प्रयोग की रोक पर अथवा निःशस्त्रीकरण के प्रयासों पर चर्चा करें, आवाज बुलंद करे। U.N.O. के इस प्रकार को जेनेवा फोरम का नाम दिया गया।

4. U.N.O. के निःशस्त्रीकरण हेतु किये गये प्रयास

U.N.O. में एक विभाग की संयुक्त राष्ट्र निःशस्त्रीकरण सम्बन्धी मामलों का विभाग (U.N. Department for Disarmament

परम्परागत शस्त्रों में जमीन, हवा एवं समुन्दर सम्बन्धी शस्त्र आते है। यह विभाग इन शस्त्रों से (सैनिक उपकरण) सम्बन्धित आंकड़े जुटाने का कार्य करता है।

(अ) छोटे उपकरणों पर रोक :–

छोटे उपकरणों पर रोक लगाने हेतु भी U.N. Programme of Action to Prevent Combat and Eradicate The Illicit Trade in Small Arms and Light Weapons in All Aspects की स्थापना न्यूयार्क में जुलाई 2001 में की गयी। पुनः इसकी बैठक 2003 में भी हुई पर कोई संतोषजनक परिणाम प्राप्त नहीं हुआ।

इन गैर कानूनी शस्त्रों ने मानव शांति एवं सुरक्षा को लगातार चोट पहुँचायी है अतः इनकी समाप्ति का प्रयास भी आज की बड़ी आवश्यकता है। आज जो आतंकवाद एवं हिंसक आंतकवादी घटनाऐं देखने सुनने में आती है उनका मूल कारण भी इन छोटे गैर कानूनी हिंसक उपकरणों का संग्रह एवं गुप्त वितरण ही है। नक्सलवाद इसका प्रमुख उदाहरण है।

(ब) भूमिगत बारूदी सुरंगो का अंत :–

U.N.O. ने इस दिशा में विशेष प्रयास एवं सफलता प्राप्त की है। The Antipersonnel Mine Ban Convention (APMBC) का निर्माण किया गया। प्रयास है कि U.N.O. के सदस्य राष्ट्रों द्वारा ऐसा कानून बनाकर अगले दस वर्षों में इनका समूल विनाश किया जायेगा।

(स) जनसंहार के हिंसक उपकरणों का अंत :–

U.N.O. में एक विभाग The Department of The weapons on Mass Destruction भी कार्यरत है जो नरसंहारी उपकरणों जैसे आणविक, जैविक, रासायनिक (Nuclear, Biological and Chemical)

उपकरण जैसे मिसाइल्स को समाप्त करने के लिए प्रयत्नशील है। ये कार्य Organization for The Prohibition of Chemical Weapons (OPCW) कर रहा है।

विविध संधिया (Treaties)

1. एक Comprehensive Test Ban Treaty (CTBT) आणविक हथियारों के परीक्षण पर रोक के लिए भी काम हो रहा है।
2. Treaty on The Non Proliferation of Nuclear Weapon (N.P.T.) भी बनायी गयी।
3. Chemical Weapon Conventions (C.W.C) 1997
4. Biological Weapons Conventions (B.W.C.) 1975 में बनाया गया।

5. निःशस्त्रीकरण के प्रयास एवं अध्यापक की भूमिका

शांति शिक्षा के उद्देश्यों की प्राप्ति में निःशस्त्रीकरण पर परिचर्चा अति आवश्यक है। इसमें निःशस्त्रीकरण का अर्थ समझने एवं उन उपायों पर विचार होना चाहिये जिसमें निःशस्त्रीकरण स्थानीय, राष्ट्रीय एवं अर्न्तराष्ट्रीय सभी स्तरों पर संभव हो सके। अतः इस सम्बन्ध में अध्यापक की भूमिका निम्नांकित हो सकती है–

1. अध्यापक शस्त्रीकरण की गम्भीरता से परिचर्चा करे। कुछ उदाहरण उन घटनाओं के जहाँ हिंसक उपकरणों के प्रयोग का शिकार निर्दोष नागरिकों (स्त्रियों, बच्चों) को होना पड़ा बताकर हिंसक उपकरणों के प्रति घृणा के भाव उत्पन्न करें।
2. विश्वयुद्धों पर चर्चा करें । आणविक बम विस्फोट (हिरोशिमा एवं नागासाकी की दिल दहलाने वाली

घटनाओं) पर चर्चा हो जिससे बच्चों के मन में निःशस्त्रीकरण के प्रयत्नों के प्रति सकारात्मक भाव उत्पन्न हो।

3. U.N.O. की बैठक, संसद की बैठक छात्रों से अपने स्तर पर करवा कर निःशस्त्रीकरण के प्रस्ताव पारित करवाये जायें। इस दिशा में U.N.O. के प्रयासों की जानकारी दी जाये।

4. छात्रों से इस विषय पर चर्चा की जाये की शस्त्रीकरण किस प्रकार मानव के अधिकारों एवं राष्ट्रीय, अंर्तराष्ट्रीय विकास एवं शांति के मार्ग को अवरूद्व करता है तथा मानव सुरक्षा एवं शांति के लिए निःशस्त्रीकरण के प्रयत्न पर तेजी से अमल किया जाना आज की सबसे बडी आवश्यकता है।

इस प्रकार अध्यापक शस्त्रीकरण के संकट बताकर एवं निःशस्त्रीकरण की उपयोगिता सिद्व कर छात्रों को इस हेतु किये जा रहे प्रयत्नों से जोड़ सकता है। निःशस्त्रीकरण के प्रति आस्था के भाव जागृत होने पर शांति का मार्ग निश्चय ही प्रशस्त हो सकेगा।

अध्ययन अध्यापन क्रियाऐं

1. विषय से संबंधित परिचर्चा कर इकाई की प्रस्तावना की जायेगी।

2. समाचार पत्रों से संबंधित अंशों की एकत्रीकरण कर उस पर परिचर्चा की जायेगी।

3. संबंधित मानचित्र, चार्ट, स्क्रेप बुक आदि का निर्माण करवाया जायेगा।

मूल्यांकन

1. शस्त्रीकरण किसे कहते है।
2. निःशस्त्रीकरण को परिभाषित करें।
3. विश्व समुदाय को शस्त्रीकरण से होने वाले नुकसान के उदाहरण दें।
4. शस्त्रीकरण ने किस प्रकार पारिवारिक एवं सामाजिक शांति पर प्रहार किया है।
5. U.N.O. के द्वारा निःशस्त्रीकरण के लिये किये गये उपायों को बताये।
6. यदि आप UNESCO के महासचिव होते हो इस समस्या के निदान के लिये जो कदम उठाते वे कौन कौन से होतें।
7. निःशस्त्रीकरण के लिये एक अध्यापक को विद्यालय में कौन–कौन सी शैक्षिक क्रियाएं आयोजित करनी चाहिये।